# Handbook of Concierge Medical Practice Design

"After only working in traditional primary care for 2.5 years post-residency, I already knew this was not the level of care or service I wanted to provide my patients. I'd already spent countless hours researching concierge medicine, but still had so many questions. Maria successfully guided me out of the fog and set me on a clear course to launch a successful concierge practice. I highly recommend her knowledge, expertise & creativity to anyone interested in practicing concierge medicine."

**Family Wellness Center of Charleston**
*Stania DeJesus, D.O., Owner*
*Charleston, South Carolina*

"*The Handbook of Concierge Medical Practice Design* is a well-written, concise, and on-point guide for any practicing physician contemplating starting a concierge medical practice. Maria Todd has proven again why she is a leading expert in the areas of Concierge Medicine, Branding, Consulting, Health Care, Marketing, Medical Tourism, Planning and Physician Practice Administration. She conveys her sincerest desire to see any physician wishing to pursue concierge medicine succeed by the exercises she provides in the book. A highly recommended book."

**Richard Krasner, MA, MHA**
*Blogger-n-Chief, Transforming Workers' Comp Blog*

"So glad we have a resource NOW, since Concierge Medicine is growing at the rapid pace of 30% each year. A must for any physicians thinking about converting or who have already converted their practice where it didn't quite work out like they planned.

Competing with the chain drugstores for initial diagnosis, a concierge model is always a better answer, see Chapter 4 for more insight. Also look to Chapter 6 for more details on sorting out the financials. In Chapter 9, Maria goes into detail about what qualifications to look for when choosing an EXPERT who knows Concierge Medicine. Don't get caught up with big box conversion companies, as one size does not fit all. Look also to making sure telehealth & technology are part of the offerings, making sure the money a patient pays for the subscription gives them more or better service offerings. Chapters 8 & 13 give additional guidance about product design and what to offer because simply paying more for what patients are already getting doesn't fly!"

**Arney Benson, PharmD, MBA**
*A.B. Consulting for Healthcare*

# Handbook of Concierge Medical Practice Design

Maria K. Todd

CRC Press
Taylor & Francis Group
Boca Raton London New York

CRC Press is an imprint of the
Taylor & Francis Group, an **informa** business
A PRODUCTIVITY PRESS BOOK

CRC Press
Taylor & Francis Group
6000 Broken Sound Parkway NW, Suite 300
Boca Raton, FL 33487-2742



Printed on acid-free paper
Version Date: 20141014

ISBN-13: 978-1-4665-6818-1 (pbk)



**Visit the Taylor & Francis Web site at**
**http://www.taylorandfrancis.com**

**and the CRC Press Web site at**
**http://www.crcpress.com**

# Contents

# Foreword

As physicians, most of us realize that it is becoming more difficult, if not impossible to practice primary care medicine. Primary care has been more transformed in the past 10 years than in the entire 30 years prior. As a result, more than 50% of small to medium-sized independent primary care practices have disappeared over this time, through bankruptcy, early retirement, or absorption into hospitals or larger groups. The reasons for this are multiple, but the most major factor may be the preponderance of very large deductibles, which makes going to the primary care doctor a cash expense for most patients. Compared to 10 years ago, when high deductible health plans were very unusual, today over 90% of Affordable Care Act plans and over 50% of non-ACA insurance plans now have high deductibles. Patients with a $3000 deductible may not mind paying the first $3000 for a $60,000 surgical procedure, but it is harder to get them to pay $2000 for a year of quarterly checkups, labs, and tests for their diabetes or hypertension. Due to these higher deductibles, primary care doctors are now effectively cash practices accepting insurance rates. In addition, insurance companies have become much more sophisticated at not paying for primary care. The requirement that every screening procedure we do has an associated ICD9 diagnosis code makes it difficult for primary care practices to get paid. Increasing government regulation, such as the requirement to use electronic medical records that are usually more designed for specialists than primary care, add to the burden.

Medicine has also become more sophisticated. The Institute of Medicine estimates that it takes approximately 1.25 hours a year to counsel patients on the basic preventative care needs for good quality health care. Another 45 minutes per year are spent in paperwork for a total of 2 hours per year per patient before any time is spent on additional health diagnoses. Yet the average patient is seen 3–4 times per year for 15 minute visits! This disconnect between what is needed for good primary care and the amount of time that primary care physicians have with patients is the reason for the disconnect in primary care reimbursement.

Personalized (formerly known as "concierge"), direct pay and primary care medical home practices solve this burden by allowing more time with patients and better care. I would argue that these types of practices will also help our nation's shortage of primary care physicians by allowing competent, caring MDs to spend more time with the sicker, more needy patients, while mid-level practitioners and less-experienced physicians care for the healthier and less needy.

Several studies have shown that personalized medicine practices save the health care system money, mostly by reducing the need for hospitalization. The average cost for a good health care policy for a 60-year-old couple in the United States is now about $24,000 per year. Adding another $3000/year to that for a concierge physician (or $600/year for a PCMH) is a small price to pay for the level of increased care patients receive. And often that $3000 can be made up for in savings negotiated by the physician on behalf of their patients.

Making the decision to convert to a more patient-centered practice is one of the hardest and most complex decisions a physician will make in his or her lifetime, and requires professional input and guidance. The road to going from superficial care for 2000 patients to good care for 200–600 patients is fraught with legal, financial, and strategic land mines which must be carefully navigated. Maria Todd addresses each of these issues in a way that is forthright and understandable.

I have known Maria Todd for several years and she has transformed my thinking about how primary care medicine can and should be practiced. Todd is one of the world's leading experts on concierge, medical home and direct pay practices having helped to transform the professional lives of hundreds of physicians. More than anyone I have ever met she understands the landscape of health care and what needs to be done to help physicians reinvent and build the medical practice of their dreams.

**Floyd B. Russak, MD**
*Clinical Faculty, Harvard, University of Colorado, and Rocky Vista Schools of Medicine*
*Past President, Arapahoe-Douglas-Elbert Medical Society*
*Board of Directors, Colorado Medical Society*
*Medical Director/President, East-West Health Centers*

# Preface

I remember very clearly, when I became interested in helping physicians stand up to managed care and the fear of losing their professional autonomy in favor of "cookbook" medicine written by my buddies down the hall, who are professional actuaries.

In the 1980s, one of my earliest clients (I started consulting in 1983) came to me and said, "I want a different kind of practice. I don't want to be controlled by insurance or Medicare, I want to charge cash and not be bothered with insurance, rebrand my practice to primary care, nutrition, and a bit of alternative and complementary medicine services, care for fewer patients, get to know my patients more intimately, and take as long as I need to practice medicine my way." Fast forward to 30 years later and some people are calling this trendy, concierge care, boutique medicine, direct practice, membership medicine, and a bunch of other names.

I've always been the one to find opportunities in healthcare when someone else sees a pothole in the road. I grew up in an entrepreneurial family, married an entrepreneur, and have always come up with solutions to help doctors and hospitals face the next trend, challenge, the next disaster, and the next obstacles. My clients' practices have thrived, contributed to the community, and saved lives.

Now we have a system of healthcare in America that could stop their practices from thriving and make their practice of medicine a struggle, a disappointment, and for some, even a regret of a career choice. I've had physicians, my personal physicians, call me at home, on an evening, in tears saying that they don't know what to do, they can't survive, and that they don't know how to turn things around. Their bills are all past due and they are facing bankruptcy, the staff wants raises they can't accommodate, and they haven't paid themselves in months, but they are working 90-hour weeks. One called me on a Tuesday and suffered a heart attack the following Thursday.

In another instance, a doctor called us after learning what it would cost to transition the practice to concierge medicine. His practice was out of compliance with the Health Insurance Portability and Accountability Act (HIPAA) and Health Information Technology for Economic and Clinical Health Act (HITECH), he had no electronic medical records (EMRs), he had not reviewed his managed care contracts for more than 7 years, the practice was owed more than $1.5 million in accounts receivable, and he had no credit and a bankruptcy a few years ago. He had hidden assets from the bankruptcy, which he openly admitted, had no Control of Hazardous Substances Policy, and people were tripping over themselves and clutter in the office. He elected to pay a buddy in another town $5,000 for a copy of everything the buddy's consultant prepared. That's like copying someone's algebra answers without being able to show their work. We checked back a year later and found he had sold 17 concierge memberships to patients, and received three "fan letters" from his contracted managed care plans—insisting that he quit concierge medicine or get off their panel. Were we sympathetic? Nope. Concierge medicine transition is not that easy. More physicians would transition if all it took was a document set.

I've had a doctor call me because he read someone's blog and followed that person's advice on a "Direct Practice" business model and paid the blogger over $10,000 for "consulting." The blogger guided him down a path that might have been permitted in Canada or someplace else, but was highly illegal in the United States. For his $10,000 he received a one-size-fits-all brochure, some sear engine optimization (SEO) suggestions, and a contract template. He offered his Direct Practice package for sale and the regulators came and issued an injunction to close his direct practice, insisting he was unlawfully engaged in the business of insurance. If convicted, he faces restitution to all paid-up members, a requirement to pay attorney's fees for all plaintiffs, and possible jail time and administrative penalties of not less than $5,000 for each first violation. The penalty for committing a subsequent or knowing violation can be at least $10,000 for each violation up to a maximum of $500,000, which was more than the memberships he sold and a criminal record that will impair his medical license forever. Initially, he thought that the $10,000 price for the blogger's consulting was a real bargain! Now he must also pay legal fees to defend himself, and his professional liability insurance won't cover him for defense of this criminal act. When he originally designed the practice with the blogger, he had no nefarious intent. He just wanted to offer affordable healthcare at a reasonable price.

I remember thinking, "They can't quit or give up. Medicine needs these good doctors. Managed care plans couldn't care less if they quit or thrive. But they need good counsel and it's not easy to find."

For the past 7 years, I've been helping physicians convert to concierge medicine as a business model. We've turned some practices into million-dollar membership practices. We've retooled them and found new ways to connect with patients who want something different than the typical managed care revolving-door practice. Since then I've also written many articles, blogged on concierge medicine, strategized and launched many practices, and reengineered others that were stalled, failing, or operating without measurable goals, direction, or a strategy. The work I've done with them has renewed hope, enthusiasm, and direction to develop specific plans to create fulfilling practices that thrive and serve patients. The ideas and techniques I've shared in this book are geared to reach the same objectives. I offer this book as a blueprint for transforming your practice, or in some cases, building your first practice during these tough and challenging times.

My hope is that this book will serve as a well-worn, dog-eared reference tool that you will use for years to come. I hope that you enjoy it, learn from it, and I fervently hope that you will use it to make good business decisions. Please feel free to contact me with any questions: (mtodd@mercuryadvisorygroup.com/800.727.4160). Or, take advantage of my long-standing, always-open offer to Ask Me Anything. I always offer a complimentary 15-minute curbside consult for physicians considering a transition to concierge medicine. Schedule your appointment using my self-scheduling tool at http://meetme.so/MariaTodd. Finally, please visit my website (http://MercuryAdvisoryGroup.com) to find downloadable supplemental tools, worksheets, white papers, articles and blog posts of interest to concierge physicians. Or follow me on LinkedIn, Twitter @AskMariaTodd and @Concierge Docs, or Reddit—http://reddit.com/r/AskMariaTodd.

**Maria Todd**

# About the Author

**Maria Todd** is an award-winning and internationally respected healthcare business consultant. She frequently presents continuing education workshops, seminars, and keynote addresses for international, national, state, and regional healthcare organizations, investment firms, pharmaceutical and device manufacturers, and medical staff meetings.

She has been consulting and managing medical groups in healthcare since shortly after graduation. She's intimately familiar with the brand-building power of a successful marketing strategy and leading-edge innovation in healthcare. She built her first concierge medical practices and amenities-based practices internationally in the 1990s. They simply weren't called *concierge* then; they were called private practices because the alternative was the public health, single-payer system. Maria often says, "If you wait long enough, you see things rotate back through again. I see cycles and recycles in healthcare (like independent practice associations [IPAs], and accountable care organizations [ACOs], for example). We'll continue to see it until someone breaks the mold. *Grab a hammer!*"

Maria is the author of several commercially published, peer-reviewed books on myriad topics in healthcare business management, including the industry's top books on managed care, physician employment contracting, physician integration and alignment, medical tourism, and this latest title on concierge medicine. Her work is easily found on the Internet.

Maria strives to be accessible to individual practitioners. She maintains a popular website that attracts more than 1,000 visitors a day and provides training through her website and private workshops and webinars. She blogs regularly at http://mercuryadvisorygroup.com, contributes actively on LinkedIn, and works one-on-one with clinicians across the country and throughout the world. Through her consulting firm, Mercury Advisory Group, she has been instrumental in building concierge medical practices, clinics, and hospitals throughout the United States and abroad. She also works on healthcare projects in the developing world, primarily in Asia and Africa.

Her clients benefit from dozens of checklists, templates, and worksheets that can bring order out of the chaos that accompanies most concierge medicine transition and marketing/promotion projects.

## Chapter 1

# Private Practice in Transition

## Introduction

People who care about helping others have historically been drawn to medicine and healthcare. I started on a path toward medical school and an accident while working as a volunteer firefighter on a glorious Sunday afternoon in 1979 thwarted those plans. I found I could still be involved in the business of healthcare in other ways instead of standing at the operating table. Most physicians desire clinical autonomy, enjoy collegial relationships with other practitioners, take pride in their work, bring home a good income, and revel in creativity and flexibility when they establish a private practice. Those who work for others sometimes grumble and complain that these rewards are sometimes stifled as an employee, but they realize they traded security for their freedoms.

I view the role of most concierge medicine physicians as healing artist, counselor, and entrepreneur. Concierge physicians feel proud and humble. They have access to a new dimension of relationships and engagement with patients from all walks of life. No more seven-minute visits, less frustration, more delight in the practice of medicine. With each visit, they improve healthcare, one visit at a time.

### *The Exciting New World of Medical Practice*

What has changed medical practice through the evolution of concierge medicine are the rules of engagement. The terms of the deal place more emphasis on marketing, social media, promotion, building a brand, establishing authority, and finding the "extras" that differentiate the concierge medical practice from all others. It brings a marketable product to people of moderate means. The people get to decide if they are willing to pay additional money for the product. The customers dictate to the physician what meets *their* requirements as a *minimum viable product* (*MVP*). I tell my clients, "If they won't buy it, it's a concept and not a product. It only graduates to being a product when people will pay money for it."

## The Disruption of the Traditional Private Medical Practice in America

> The majority of physicians believe health reform will increase their patient loads while decreasing the financial viability of their practices.
>
> **—Meritt Hawkins Survey, 2012**

Healthcare insurance reform in America is a confusing, expensive, and multidimensional moving target. It has lots of moving parts, some not well developed despite the good intentions of its authors. It has many effects on the practice of medicine and the business of healthcare delivery in America.

The majority of America's physicians view healthcare reform as largely intrusive into what's best for their patients. They can appreciate that patients are more likely to seek care if they have insurance to protect them from financial ruin, and they appreciate that insurance plans now cover an annual checkup and at least talk the talk of the importance of prevention to reduce or mitigate the risks associated with chronic disease. However, they don't like how the healthcare insurance reforms were executed.

As a result, many physicians intend to change the way that they practice medicine and change their practice patterns in ways that might reduce access to care for some patients. Others plan to retire early, work part time, or adopt other business models to continue private practice.

It is believed by many of the healthcare business analysts that full-time, independent practitioners who presently participate with third-party payment plans will largely be supplanted by employed, part-time, locum tenens, and concierge practitioners.

In a 2012 survey of more than 14,000 physicians who own their own practices, 9.6% plan to start direct pay or concierge medicine practices in the next 1 to 3 years. The movement is across all medical disciplines with 6.8% of all physicians planning to stop taking insurance in favor of concierge-style medicine or so-called *direct primary care*.

Meanwhile, many new physicians completing their residencies are also heading straight to concierge or direct practice models and bypassing the traditional practice model altogether. A significant number of hospitalists, whose employment contracts are up for renewal, are also moving to concierge and direct practice models, rather than renewing their employment agreement with the hospitalist groups.

Three trends are emerging in this departure from the traditional managed care participating practices.

## Concierge Medicine

In *concierge medicine*, the physician develops an amenities-rich membership program, and collects a monthly or annual membership fee to pay for the amenities program in addition to the medical services rendered. In order to render the membership amenities, and practice medicine at a different pace and with a different doctor-patient relationship, without the productivity requirements of medicine and administrative paperwork associated with managed care contractual obligations for paperwork and reporting beyond claims submission that are required in the traditional practice. Many still accept insurance allowable amounts for covered services, but may not be under contract with the health plans. This enables the patient to enjoy the use of their healthcare insurance benefits, albeit "out-of-network" but the physician is not required to write off balances unpaid by the insurer, and it allows the physician the freedom to charge what they want for the services they provide at the level they choose to render service. Not all concierge medical practices accept insurance or file for reimbursement on behalf of their members.

Consider this comparison. The insurer covers the purchase of a pen. The allowable amount affords the insured person to purchase an inexpensive, basic stick pen, that averages about $1.29 in any office supply or discount department store. It writes. It works, but it is not the same as a Mont Blanc Meisterstück Solitaire Doué Geometric Dimension Classique Rollerball, which runs about $700. Even if the person submits a receipt, all they are going to receive as a benefit is $1.29. As a published author and international speaker, it is my preference to use my Mont Blanc Meisterstück Solitaire Doué Geometric Dimension Classique Rollerball pen to sign my books at a book signing. I like the way it feels in my hand, I like the way it glides across the paper effortlessly, which is important since I do a lot of writing.

I like what it reflects about my personal brand when I am in public—the mark of success and importance, and it is what others expect of my brand when I sign a contract or a book. People purchase concierge medicine membership amenities in much the same way.

Managed care participating practices are by their very nature *volume driven*. The discount accepted by managed care providers is in lieu of having to do their own marketing and promotion. Instead, they accept a discounted rate in exchange for the health plan steering patients to their door. I have trouble understanding why physicians complain about the rates they are paid for these services. If they had to do all their own marketing and promotion to capture market share, they might see less volume, and it might cost them more per patient encounter to risk the money they spend on marketing. That's because most physicians were never educated in marketing techniques and have no clue how to go about it. What they are doing when they write off managed care reductions without allocating the discounts to "marketing" expense makes no sense to me. It says right in most contracts, "Plan shall use its best efforts to market the Physician." The plan also maintains websites that list the physician, refer callers on the phone to physicians, print directories that list the physician, and offer discounted rates to plan members who select participating physicians, while punishing the plan members for using out-of-network physicians with a higher deductible and higher cost share. Those are marketing efforts. The branding efforts are still the responsibility of the physician so that there is some differentiation among all the providers on the list. I guess most physicians (and their practice managers) missed that memo.

So essentially, these volume-driven practices must figure out how to deliver high-quality, safe healthcare and fulfill all the obligations of managed care participation (lots of administrative reporting, etc.) and still manage the volume of patient visits and medical services it takes to make the numbers work each month. That's the business model—plain and simple. It's not good or bad; it's just different from what concierge medicine is all about. One has to sell a lot of stick ballpoint pens to equal the sale of one Mont Blanc Meisterstück Solitaire Doué Geometric Dimension Classique Rollerball—about 542 to be exact. And not everyone is in the market for the Mont Blanc. While most everyone needs a writing instrument, some prefer Lamy, or Waterman, or Cross, and some prefer a Mont Blanc that is more understated, like the Mont Blanc Meisterstück Classique Rollerball or Ball point, or the next level up, the fountain pen. Those are just different brands within a class of writing instruments.

## Direct Practice

The direct practice model (as in "direct to the consumer without interference of a middleman or insurer") is a model whereby the physician accepts cash only in payment for services rendered, and resigns all contracts with insurers. This often includes resignation from the Medicare program.

That resignation is really a bigger decision than most realize, because if it doesn't work out, the physician has a tougher time than the parable of the Prodigal Son (Luke 15:12) in a sense. They can leave, but coming back requires a waiting period, an application, all new vetting, the expense of new contract analysis and negotiation, and if one is no longer a participating Medicare provider, and in good standing, one may not be able to rejoin the ranks of the participating managed care providers. (And there's no coat of many colors or a celebratory dinner, either!) To rejoin Medicare, for example, requires a two-year "time out" period.

This could result in significant difficulty capturing market share, especially in a market downturn. Patients with health insurance that pays at some level for covered services, however small, want to derive value from the premiums they pay for insurance. Now that some policies have no out-of-network benefits, a prudent shopper might be swayed to purchase a membership in a concierge practice where there is some chance to be able to receive at least a pittance in reimbursement for office visits and other diagnostic services rather than nothing at all.

Some direct practices have been developed based on a flawed strategy that they can offer unlimited health benefits for a monthly membership fee. In many instances, this is both illegal, as it too closely resembles a regulated, prepaid health plan known as a health maintenance organization (HMO), but without having the authority to operate such a business, and it is also financially imprudent, because the physician often does not purchase reinsurance to cover the excess losses that could arise from rendering more care and amenities services than the membership covers each month.

To offer a product without the regulatory authority to do so is illegal in most states, is not financially sustainable, and could eventually give rise to default. The default occurs because the physician cannot render as much service as that which the member patients require, and as a result they start to scale back, or have to close down the practice because costs exceed revenues.

Think of this as an all-you-can-eat seafood buffet, like the ones in Atlantic City and Las Vegas. Crab, shrimp, African and Maine lobster, diver scallops, clams, mussels, halibut, salmon, and more. One day the manager comes to the chef and says, "We're upside down here—take it down a notch," so the chef first reduces a few items that were on the menu, but were often passed over for other delicacies, the first step in cost containment. The manager comes back again and says "cut back more." This time, the chef removes a few items. Perhaps the chef replaces these items with other items to fill the gap on the display but with a new dish that uses a less expensive ingredient, say tuna tetrazzini (tuna casserole—made with tuna, spaghetti, Parmesan cheese, and mushrooms). You get the idea.

Eventually, though the buffet is still hobbling along in operation, the buffet's brand suffers a breach of brand promise and the market goes someplace else. Trust is a big deal in branding, and what the regulators want to avoid, and why the Certificate of Authority comes only after review of financial status and actuarial assumptions that align to reasonable premium pricing. This is largely because the regulators don't want to spend money they don't have in their budget each year answering consumer complaints and enforcing the regulations because the buffet no longer offers or delivers on what was originally promised and sold. Since the regulators also require the admitted and authorized health insurers and plans to undergo these rigors at great annual and quarterly expense, they also don't want to catch flack from the health plans that could argue successfully that the physician in the direct practice model is engaged in unfair competition with them.

And one last thought: If you believe that putting a little disclaimer on a direct practice offer, contract, or advertisement that states "*this is not an offer of insurance*" is the solution, I have this bridge from LA to Hawaii that is currently seeking investors ….

## Corporate Concierge Medicine

This term has been applied to describe several different business models of concierge medicine. In some instances, it refers to the franchise models available from MDVIP and SignatureMD, among others. Another is MedLion, which charges consumers $59 a month and $10 per visit to join a network of clinics. There is no exclusivity and two MedLion participating providers could be located across the street from each other, or even in the same office complex. The consumer has the right to choose any provider. No insurance is accepted for payment, and participating providers don't bill insurance plans—not as a courtesy, not at all. The argument in defense of this model is that not having to bill insurance reduces overhead by about 40% each year. It also eliminates the marketing service that the insurance plans include, so while they physician no longer has the 40% administrative expense of billing insurance as a contractual obligation, they must now spend possibly more money on marketing, brand differentiation, brand visibility, and customer retention.

The other key difference in these practices is that the membership contract is held in the name of the corporation, not the participating physician. If the physician chooses to break the relationship, he or she must start again and abandon the members who have paid their membership to the corporate entities that hold the membership contracts. In addition, there may be noncompete, noncircumvention, and time and distance restrictions present within the participation agreement. The physician may be able to connect with the existing member patients, but only if those patients come to the physician of their own volition, and cancel and possibly forfeit the remaining months of membership dues to do so. Meanwhile, the physicians also place themselves in a competitive lineup with other concierge practices, and may not be able to compete with the volume-based model of the corporate concierge practices, that have a running start, reciprocity, portability, and more.

Some of these corporate concierge programs are working with insurers to incorporate concierge membership benefits into the benefit program, but upon careful scrutiny, that arrangement may reflect on the insurance program's brand as an amenity, instead of the physician's brand. Cigna is one of the insurers developing such a model, and Qliance is one of several concierge brands that are forging relationships with insurers and helping them build a benefits package that incorporates their services.

The physicians who choose this approach to their future as a private practice owner often do so without fully understanding the impact of their decision. They often make an emotional and reactive decision without fully weighing the implications of what they might face in the following three to five years, if they decide they want to leave the corporate model and build their own brand instead of the corporate brand. They may find that the consulting and transition costs that they avoided in adopting the corporate model were not avoided at all, but merely delayed to their detriment. I say that because if they don't own the membership contracts and cannot access those members, they've merely sidestepped the transition of their own practice to the benefit of the franchise owners. They begin again with nothing other than their practice equipment assets and no existing transitional market share. This is especially true if they jettisoned the patients that once trusted them in the traditional medical practice—especially if they jettisoned those patients in a way that angered the patients and burned bridges.

## The Patient-Centered Medical Home

The patient-centered medical home (PCMH) concept is not new. What is new about it is that the model was recognized as a part of the American healthcare reform law. The law includes medical home demonstration projects for Medicare and Medicaid but several insurance plans have also embraced it and are now actively contracting with physicians who are prepared to work within this business model. The concept, in which a physician leads a team of clinicians in the delivery and coordination all of a patient's healthcare services, has shown that it can reduce costs, improve care, and even potentially decrease clinician burnout.

The medical home has been endorsed by four medical societies and propelled forward by the Patient-Centered Primary Care Collaborative, a coalition of large employers, insurers, consumer groups, and doctors. For many physicians, at least at the surface, this is a logical next step in improving patient care and one that a growing number of practices are expected to take postreform. What they may not realize at first is the cost involved in developing an *accredited* PCMH.

To be able to track patient procedures and their outcomes, an electronic medical record and an advanced functionality website and patient access portal are key components. This model takes a higher level of practice management than is found in most private primary care practices in America. Physician compensation changes too. In the PCMH, physicians are compensated based on productivity, with a small bonus distributed for patient outcomes, amounting to only 1% to 2% of salary. The physicians may also receive another component part of their salary that comes from performing certain administrative tasks, with an accounting system that establishes a relative value system (RVS) with relative value units (RVUs) assigned to various nonclinical tasks that are necessary to operate the practice.

Insurers that contract with physicians for medical home care delivery are often contracted in a mixed reimbursement model. Some money may be advanced or carved out to enable the practice to afford additional nurse practitioners or physician assistants or registered nurses who act as care coordinators to perform case management or care navigation. An advanced information system and predictive modeling tool is expensive but mission critical to monitor chronic disease and campaign patients with engagement activities to take a more personal, participative role in their preventive care, while at the same time enabling the nurses and physicians to view the data in a predictive model versus a reactive management mode.

Payer contract terms in the PCMH model tend to be 2 to 3 years in duration, and often share risk, enabling the physician to retain a portion of the savings generated by the practice. These contracts require an experienced, sharp eye for analysis and expertise negotiating shared risk and capitated contracts, along with pay-for-performance or as more recently renamed, *value-based* reimbursement schemes. The benchmarks for every performance metric should be clearly spelled out in an attachment to the contract for the sake of fair dealings and transparency. Otherwise, the physicians face the risk of contracting for illusive bonuses and ambiguous rewards that might never materialize. The greatest risk here is that the front-end cost of PCMH establishment and staffing spent in anticipation of realizing non-specific bonuses and benefits could bring about a bankruptcy if the plan doesn't negotiate a kick-start allowance with the practice to help fund the front-end startup costs.

The electronic medical records software requirements in the PCMH setting are much more advanced because they often include the ability to perform natural language searches of entries as well as structured data searches to identify tests or processes that are missing or late, and standing order sets that prompt physicians to consider particular *evidence-based* procedures or tests when a patient presents with abnormal lab values or a particular condition.

What is interesting is that this orientation toward a powerful electronic medical record is actually contrary to the orientation of physicians in the direct and concierge practice model, who believe that the electronic medical record is an unnecessary expense tied to American health insurance reform. We find this ilk more along the faction that wants to resign from Medicare and all insurance programs, and simply operate a small cash practice for a limited number of patients. They also want nothing to do with e-prescribing, ICD-10 preparation, or Health Insurance Portability and Accountability Act (HIPAA) and Health Information Technology for Economic and Clinical Health Act (HITECH) compliance.

My point here is not castigation for their choices. I defend their right to choose how they run their business, and ultimately, they need little in the form of transitional practice development services; they just need our medical practice marketing and branding experts to help them figure out a strategy to sell their differentiated products. There are some physicians all around the country who have established practices and are paid $25,000 to $30,000 per year to be the personal physician of politicians, movie stars, and corporate executives. They may limit their practice to 50 patients per year. While it is difficult to find 50 patients that want that and are willing to pay those rates, they do exist. The key is connecting to that target market if that's the strategy one has chosen.

## Accreditation and Practice Management for the Private Medical Practice of Tomorrow

Practices must meet certain accreditation criteria to become a recognized or accredited patient-centered medical home. This is not a designation that one can just slap onto a tag line on a logo or brochure, though many try it and get away with it—but not for long. Practices that attempt to use this term are quickly admonished by contracting agencies that will share in the costs of startup. No accreditation, no contract.

To achieve the first level in the Physician Practice Connections—Patient-Centered Medical Home requirements, a provider must achieve 25 to 49 points of 100 possible points in the following nine standards. To achieve Level 3, the practice must reach at least 75 points in enactment of these standards. Accreditation is conferred by the National Committee for Quality Assurance (NCQA). There are fees associated with purchasing the standards, and for the accreditation survey itself, as well as for the travel and accommodation costs of the surveyors. The accreditation standards for PCMH and the scoring information is as follows:

### *NCQA Scoring Criteria for Patient-Centered Medical Homes*[*]

#### *Standard 1: Access and Communication—9 Possible Points*

A. Has written standards for patient access and patient communication.* 4 possible points
B. Uses data to show it meets its standards for patient access and communication.* 5 possible points

[*] An asterisk (*) indicates a must-pass element.

### *Standard 2: Patient Tracking and Registry Functions—21 Possible Points*

A. Uses data system for basic patient information (mostly nonclinical data). 2 possible points
B. Has clinical data system with clinical data in searchable fields. 3 possible points
C. Uses the clinical data system. 3 possible points
D. Uses paper or electronic-based charting tools to organize clinical information.* 6 possible points
E. Uses data to identify important diagnoses and conditions in practice.* 4 possible points
F. Generates lists of patients and reminds patients and clinicians of services needed (population management). 3 possible points

### *Standard 3: Care Management—20 Possible Points*

A. Adoption and implementation of evidence-based guidelines for three chronic conditions.* 3 possible points
B. Generates reminders about preventative services for clinicians. 4 possible points
C. Uses nonphysician staff to manage patient care. 3 possible points
D. Conducts care management, including care plans, assessing progress, addressing barriers. 5 possible points
E. Coordinates care/follow-up for patients who receive care in inpatient and outpatient facilities. 5 possible points

### *Standard 4: Patient Self-Management Support—6 Possible Points*

A. Assesses language preference and other communication barriers. 2 possible points
B. Actively supports patient self-management.* 4 possible points

### *Standard 5: Electronic Prescribing—8 Possible Points*

A. Uses electronic system to write prescriptions. 3 possible points
B. Has electronic prescription writer with safety checks. 3 possible points
C. Has electronic prescription writer with cost checks. 2 possible points

### *Standard 6: Test Tracking—13 Possible Points*

A. Tracks tests and identifies abnormal results systematically.* 7 possible points
B. Uses electronic system to order and retrieve tests and flag duplicate tests. 6 possible points

### *Standard 7: Referral Tracking—4 Possible Points*

A. Tracks referrals using paper-based or electronic system.* 4 possible points

### *Standard 8: Performance Reporting and Improvement—15 Possible Points*

A. Has written standards for patient access and patient communication.* 3 possible points
B. Measures clinical and/or service performances by physician or across practice.* 3 possible points
C. Survey of patients' care experience. 3 possible points
D. Reports performance across the practice or by physician.* 3 possible points
E. Sets goals and takes action to improve performance. 3 possible points
F. Produces reports using standard measures. 2 possible points
G. Transmits reports with standardized measure electronically to external entities. 1 possible point

### *Standard 9: Advanced Electronic Communications—4 Possible Points*

A. Availability of interactive website (advanced functionality patient portal—beyond the traditional website).* 1 possible point
B. Electronic patient identification. 2 possible points
C. Electronic care management support (mobile health technology adoption such as *MeVisit* or similar tools). 1 possible point

In order to qualify for these three levels of PCMH Designation, a practice must pass the survey as follows:

* This website can cost upward of $50,000 to build and maintain—for just one point!

| *Level of Qualifying* | *Points* | *Must Pass Elements at 50%* |
|---|---|---|
| Level 3 | 75–100 Points | 10 of 10 |
| Level 2 | 50–74 Points | 10 of 10 |
| Level 1 | 25–49 Points | 5 of 10 |

Too often we notice physicians stating that they *are* a medical home because that's how they fancy themselves. The patient-centered medical home is not a marketing designation that one tacks onto a slogan or logo. I would bet that eventually, to use this phrase to describe one's orientation to medical practice without having the accreditation to do so will be about the same as claiming one is an accredited hospital when the hospital has not undergone and passed a survey.

To prepare for a direct contract that gives financial incentives to patients to choose PCMH medical practices for their care, the clinic needs to align primary care and specialist physicians outside the clinic. Physicians who provide care outside the accredited clinic must be contracted to follow the written protocols and their credentials vetted and privileges granted by the clinic. This arrangement of networking is necessary in the event patient demand exceeds capacity under a contracted arrangement. This alignment is more complex than simply sending patients to outside physicians, both from financial and quality management perspectives. I am one of very few consultants in the country who has the skill and experience to build a PCMH practice from the ground up and excel with this level of risk contracting. These arrangements are now referred to as *medical neighborhoods* and the transformation consultants who are competent to develop the PCMHs and medical neighborhoods are frequently referred to as practice facilitators (PFs) by agencies such as the Agency for Healthcare Research and Quality (AHRQ).

Many of those you will encounter purporting to be transition consultants are actually former practice managers who have never managed an integrated health system before, nor have they had much experience in contracting at shared risk with payers and employers. Others whom you will encounter may simply have a marketing background without the necessary healthcare administration background. As such, they may assume incorrectly that the medical practice is fully developed and ready with a product to go to market, while plain and simply not knowing what they don't know. Unfortunately, the physicians who also don't know how to procure consulting services and vet consultants or specify deliverables could be sold a contract that, in the end, won't meet their needs or deliver a sustainable concierge, direct practice, or an accredited and qualified patient-centered medical home and accompanying functional medical neighborhood. Still others will seek out a website consultant who has no clue how to deliver the interoperability of an electronic medical record with predictive modeling capabilities and natural language search capability, a practice management software program that is HIPAA and HITECH compliant, and a secure patient self-management portal mounted atop a medical practice website.

In later-stage efforts, most PCMH clinics build an alignment strategy to work closely with a particular hospital. In a fee-for-service market, the push to align doesn't exist. Global risk-based payments for inpatient and outpatient care may happen eventually, but probably not for some years to come.

## Welcome to the Disruptors' World

For my clients who have been disruptors for decades, this is not the new world, this is *their* world. They thrive in the exhilaration of reaching their goals and practicing medicine *their* way. They have identified and developed their *market niche*. For my international clients, this is simply called private practice, and the only thing new-fangled about it is the membership subscription fee. They ask me almost weekly, "What's all this noise about concierge medicine? We've been practicing medicine like that for years. We just haven't been doing the marketing part on social media or the membership fees." This is because in some countries, much the same as it was in the 1970s in the United States, physicians are prohibited by law from advertising their services. Interestingly, they still manage to deliver healthcare in the style of concierge medicine. You think not? Think about the Middle East for a moment. You don't believe there are some concierge amenities being paid for? Think about the rich oil and gas magnates in Africa and the oligarchs in the former Soviet Union. Still dubious? Go ahead, believe what you want. We are the *caboose* on this business model.

## Physician Entrepreneurship

Wikipedia defines entrepreneurship as "a process of identifying and starting a business venture, sourcing and organizing the required resources and taking both the risks and rewards associated with the venture." In 1991, I called on the University of Colorado's School of Medicine to offer to teach a class on practice management and business development for interns and residents. My offer was rejected by the dean, who responded with, "They can learn that after they leave here. We have a limited amount of time to get them the skills that they need to become doctors." He was entitled to his point of view. It is apparent that his point of view was shared by many other decision makers in many training programs around the country. But like a 1965 Bob Dylan song, these times, they are a-changin'.

Despite the lack of business management training in most medical education programs, there is a great need for business, marketing, and public relations skills for physicians. The changes in this new world of medical practice require these skills as essential tools to be able to rise up and out of the clenches of consigning all patient steerage to managed care plans and their restrictions and dictates about what is acceptable and deemed medically necessary for patients.

Now in 2014, about 17,000 physicians across the United States have proven that they can live without managed care—and the parade keeps getting longer. This year, in our practice, we have received more calls per month to transition established medical practices to concierge medicine and launch brand new ones than all the calls combined in previous years. The calls in 2014 have also been more desperate since the trend began to rise in about 2009. Is it just that we are better at marketing? Or has the number of physicians moving to or considering concierge medicine increased? It is probably a combination of both.

When these calls come, I hear anger, fear, denial, retaliation, and other emotions in the voices of the physicians. Some I want to work with, others I want to avoid and send them to my rivals with a big red ribbon on their heads. Those whom I don't want to work with won't make it until they work out their issues a little more. Nothing I can say or do or suggest will change that until they change their perspective, raise their commitment to change, and focus less on getting rich quick. These negative emotions and avariciousness will keep them from moving beyond the demolition of private practice under HMO and PPO feeder-stream practices and healthcare reform.

Those who move forward with the right strategies will succeed, while others who lack a real strategy and just launch reactively will fail with a "thud." I've witnessed a few of those too. They are the ones who offer their email and phone number for between $800–$1,200 per year and not much else. For those who offer nothing else, I believe it is all about the money.

There's no crime in that. You could call it a "different" strategy, but they should read and research the market a little more—not all models and all offers will thrive. The others with better prognoses all exhibit many common denominators, starting with a viable concierge medicine product. They will enjoy a revitalized version of private practice that is honest, lucrative, confidential, and once again delight in the practice of medicine and taking care of people.

## Building the Practice of Your Dreams

If you want to build the practice of your dreams, you will need two essential ingredients. First and foremost, you must be creative and have the ability to embrace new technology and change. You can be cautious, but you can't fear change.

You will find yourself outside your comfort zone for a bit during the transition. Every small business owner faces consternation and anxiety on a daily basis. Our cortisol pump is on overdrive. There are good consultants with professional skills in marketing, business development, sales training, public relations, advertising and branding, who can serve as good coaches or manage the business on an outsourced, contracted basis. What they cannot do for you is practice medicine.

Second, you must think like an entrepreneur—a balance of risk and reward, where challenges and the problems of health delivery turn into opportunities and potential products and services as solutions. My goal for this book is to give you a better understanding of the processes involved in the introduction of new healthcare-related products and services and to identify ways to improve and accelerate innovation in medical practice and health delivery that benefits patients through better care. (Hint: There's a mission statement and vision statement lurking about in that sentence!)

Set aside the notion that nobody wants to spend money on healthcare. If you don't believe me, go park the car in front of a massage therapy clinic and watch the traffic. Go stand in the vitamin store and watch the purchases at the checkout lines. Then go to the organic grocer and watch the checkout lines. At Whole Foods, for example, there are tables or counter stools where you can buy a coffee just in front of the registers. "Sit a spell" is the idiom they use in the south where I grew up.

We do custom research for clients through our practice. Our research consultants, economists, and statisticians are available to plan, design, and coordinate every aspect of your concierge medical practice market research project and place the final analysis in context of your specific needs. Alternatively, you can do some simple market research, free and easy, investing just your time on a day off. Observe who is buying, the accessories they carry, their watches, their shoes, what is being purchased, and how much is being spent on healthful foods, vitamins, supplements, and health and beauty aids. These customers are spending money on the things they believe will make their lives better. They are doing all this with discretionary income, and few are doing it with food stamps or coupons from the Sunday paper. The research and data gathering is simple, and the interpretation of the data you collect is something you can discuss with a consultant. Will this person buy from you? How can you know for sure? An exercise made up of a panel of your existing patients is one way to find out, using a Delphi method exercise. We do them all the time. They cost very little to do in comparison with other less-accurate ways of predictive analysis for concierge medicine. More on that in Chapter 6, Exercise 8.

Imagine what would happen in the concierge medicine world if the public saw this healthcare delivery model as a way to spend their discretionary income on something they perceive to be better care, better service, and a better product. If you can also embrace this change in perspective, perhaps you'll begin to see how marketing your practice and your products and services can be more like a public service than advertising. I dare you to walk with me and see if I can change your perception about private practice and inspire greater enthusiasm for the opportunities that await you in concierge medicine.

## What Skills Will You Need?

You may be surprised to learn that what the "B" school graduates studied can be adapted to building a thriving clinical practice. You can come out from behind the charts and the little spinning stool in the exam room and meet people and get to know the community a little better. Let them see just how close you are to a modern-day replica of that nostalgic image of the doctor depicted in the old Norman Rockwell paintings. Let your creativity flow. It is the key to building a *living brand* that explains to people what is unique about you and the ethos of your practice. Let the people see it. I will address more about living brands in Chapter 7.

My role as a consultant is to inspire you, to nudge you a little, to coach you in the areas where you are weak or unsure and turn those weaknesses into strengths and confidence. I want you to envisage concierge medicine as a delight and a creative outlet to build the practice that gets you excited to go in to work each day.

I will share ideas with you and the techniques and steps to implement them, in an ethical and effective way that enables marketing, advertising, promotion, and public relations in a classy way that works to bring in new patients. In each chapter, I promise to share a skill, a method, or an idea that can be implemented to help you not only plan a good concierge practice, but also thrive in a highly competitive setting. I have included several tools including examples, worksheets, model forms, paper-and-pen exercises, and even assignments you will be required to do to get your concierge practice off to a solid start. Little by little, page by page, you will learn new skills and new techniques by doing them.

## Marshalling the Courage and Skills to Transform Your Medical Practice

We've all read the Serenity Prayer:

> God, grant me the serenity to accept the things I cannot change,
> The courage to change the things I can,
> And wisdom to know the difference.

Do you have the courage to change the things you can? Do you even know which things need changing? Do you have the patience and perseverance to move forward? Do you have a bit of a financial cushion or the credit rating to obtain a line of credit in case you need it to ease your transition, if necessary? Without cash in hand, the stress may be too difficult or you may be tempted to consider copying someone else's consultant work product—like taking their leftover prescription medication.

I won't oversimplify: Rebranding and relaunching a revised business model has associated costs, even if you don't use a consultant. In this book, there are many ways you can cut costs on consulting and hire only the help you really need. But first, you must commit to learning some new skills that you will need to help your concierge practice to thrive. Here are a few of the skills we'll explore:

- Marketing: How will you communicate the value of your concierge product and medical services to new prospective and current patients, to be able to sell those products and services?
- Advertising: How will you convey the message to the masses?
- Branding: What is unique about what you do and how you do it? What do others think of when they think about your business and what you do? How do they describe what you do to others?
- Public Relations: How will you maintain a favorable public image for yourself and your concierge practice in the community? How will you explain this new business model in a way that doesn't come off as snobbish, highbrow, or posh, and makes the practice open and accessible to all who see the value in a different delivery model for private practice?
- Service Line Expansion: You may be interested to add new services that you previously didn't have the time to offer. Things like stem cell therapies and regenerative medicine, bio-mimetic and bio-identical hormone and anti-aging therapies, alternative and complementary medicine, genetic and molecular medicine treatment approaches that offer a personalized care plan that includes predictive testing and screening, preventive measures, and more participative engagement by patients in their health and wellness.

If while you are reading this book, you find yourself paralyzed by anger or fear, put it down. Take a break. Take a walk. Think about what you'd like the practice you've built to become. Write it down. Transitioning to concierge medicine is not an act of defiance. The transition is transformation; running to opportunity, rebirth, and one that will return you to clinical autonomy and ensure your economic viability as a small business owner.

## Reinventing Private Practice

Knowledge can reduce your stress as you go through this transition. I promise to share with you ways to attract new patients and build the loyalty of established patients by means that are ethical, tasteful, and effective. That doesn't mean that every solution I offer will work in every instance and every market. But overall, you'll find the balance that works for your particular situation. My goal is to integrate the healing and medical services you provide with the amenities-based membership product in a manner that delights you, your patients, and your family—because you'll end up being more emotionally available to all three.

While other physicians are frozen like a deer in the headlights, or hindered by anger and fear, I plan to keep you preoccupied with goal setting, planning, and implementing action steps to move forward. Think of yourself like the duck on the pond. On the surface, seemingly just floating along serene, clear, strong, resilient, and self-assured. People expect that. They expect their doctor to have an ego. But underneath, the fear, the trepidation, the anger, the doubting will have you pedaling as fast as you can toward the other side of the pond. When you make this transition to concierge medicine, you really won't *owe* anyone an explanation about your business decision to transition your practice to concierge medicine.

> Never explain yourself. Your friends don't need it and your enemies won't believe it.
>
> **—Belgicia Howell**

Your communication of your product and services will speak for itself. In fact, if you start explaining, you may leak too much of your strategy to the guy or gal who may decide to become your competitor. All your careful planning and strategy will then be up for imitation or create the threat of substitution and rivalry. Remain tightlipped about your transition prior to your launch announcement. In fact, I encourage all clients to have their staff sign a confidentiality and nondisclosure agreement specific to the transition to concierge medicine. This way, the public hears of the rebranding when you feel you are ready and able to describe the product and communicate its value and benefits. In some practices, staff members have refused to sign. Get rid of them. They are not loyal and pose a great liability.

In one example, while the doctor was planning the transition, a staffer was poisoning the well with gossip outside the practice. They didn't understand what the concierge business model was all about, so they began talking in the community about how the practice was going posh, and only going to cater to "rich people." Patients got wind of it—at church, at clubs, at the PTA, at the homeowner's association—and they started looking for another doctor because they heard all about concierge medicine from the media. Soon chart transfer requests were being received as people preemptively found a place that the not so rich would be "welcome." The practice suffered a 35% loss prior to the official announcement of the transition. While one could argue that "those people" would not have followed the doctor to the new business model, I can argue that until they heard the product and the value, the argument is based purely on conjecture.

**Tip:** Get your staff to sign a nondisclosure agreement (NDA) that requires that they not discuss anything related to your plans or preliminary research to transition your practice.

**TOOL:** NDA Model Language

TEMPLATE

**CONFIDENTIALITY AGREEMENT**

***(Obtain appropriate legal counsel before use)***

This Confidentiality Agreement (the "Agreement") is entered into by and between **[YOUR PRACTICE NAME]** (the "Company") and ________________________ ("Employee"). The Company and Employee collectively are referred to as the "Parties."

**WHEREAS,** (a) Employee wishes to become employed by the Company or, alternatively, (b) Employee is currently employed with Company and wishes to continue Employee's employment with the Company;

**WHEREAS,** the Parties acknowledge that, while employed for the Company, Employee will obtain or has obtained knowledge regarding confidential information and trade secrets of the Company and of the Company's affiliates, including but not limited to [YOUR PRACTICE NAME(S)] (the "Affiliates"); and

**WHEREAS,** Employee and the Company have entered into this Agreement to ensure the protection of the Company's and the Affiliates' confidential information and trade secrets and to prevent damage to the Company and the Affiliates caused by Employee using or disclosing such confidential information or trade secrets.

**NOW, THEREFORE,** in consideration of the mutual covenants and promises herein contained, the receipt and sufficiency of which is acknowledged by the Parties, the Parties agree as follows:

- Confidentiality. In consideration for Employee's employment with the Company, or for continued employment with, the Company, Employee agrees as follows:
  a. For the purposes of this Agreement, "Confidential Information" means all information, data, knowledge, and know-how relating, directly or indirectly, to the Company and the Affiliates and their business of *[MEDICAL SERVICES, SURGICAL SERVICES, OTHER PROCEDURES]*, including, without limitation: (i) business models and processes; (ii) inventions, products, designs, methods, know-how, techniques, and systems, including, without limitation, surgical techniques and patient treatment protocols; (iii) proprietary information, trade secrets, proprietary forms, computer software, materials and documents, including without limitation, patient screening and tracking systems; (iv) business and marketing plans, strategies, and techniques, including without limitation branding and logo development; (v) research; (vi) patient lists and patient information; (vii) referral sources, fee schedules, pricing information, supplier/vendor lists, customer and supplier/vendor strategies and plans, contracts, agreements, and leases; (viii) financial information, investment plans, financial plans and strategies; (ix) confidential personnel or human resources data; (x) any other information having present or potential commercial value; (xi) the whole or any portion or phase of any proprietary information or trade secrets; and (xii) confidential information of any kind in possession of the Company and the Affiliates, whether developed for or by the Company or the Affiliates (including information developed by Employee), received from a third party in confidence, or belonging to others and licensed or disclosed to the Company and the Affiliates in confidence for use in any aspect of its business. Any Intellectual Property (defined below) that is not publicly available shall also constitute part of the Confidential Information. The list set forth above is not intended by the Company to be a comprehensive list of Confidential Information. All Confidential Information shall be treated as Confidential Information regardless of whether it pertains to the Company or its Affiliates or its or their clients and regardless of whether it is stamped as "confidential."
  b. Employee acknowledges that the success of the Company and the Affiliates depends in large part on the protection of the Confidential Information. Employee further acknowledges that in the course

of Employee's employment with the Company, Employee will become familiar with the Company's and the Affiliates' Confidential Information. Employee recognizes and acknowledges that the Confidential Information is a valuable, special and unique asset of the Company's and the Affiliates' businesses, access to and knowledge of which are essential to the performance of Employee's duties hereunder. Employee acknowledges that use or disclosure of the Confidential Information outside the performance of Employee's job duties for the Company would cause harm and/or damage to the Company.

c. Both during or after the term of Employee's employment by the Company, Employee agrees that Employee will not, except in the ordinary course of Employee's employment with the Company, disclose any Confidential Information to any person, firm, business, company, corporation, association, or any other entity for any reason or purpose whatsoever. Employee also agrees that Employee will not make use of any Confidential Information for Employee's own purposes or for the benefit of any person, firm, business, company, corporation, or any other entity (except the Company and the Affiliates) under any circumstances during or after the term of Employee's employment. Employee shall consider and treat as confidential all Confidential Information in any way relating to the Company's and the Affiliates' business and affairs, whether created by Employee or otherwise coming into Employee's possession before, during, or after the termination of Employee's employment. Employee shall not use or attempt to use any Confidential Information in any manner which has the possibility of injuring or causing loss, whether directly or indirectly, to the Company or the Affiliates. Employee shall not, after the termination of employment, use, disclose, or permit to be used or disclosed, any such Confidential Information, it being agreed that all such Confidential Information shall be and remain the sole and exclusive property of the Company and the Affiliates.

d. Employee shall not decompile, disassemble, or reverse engineer the Confidential Information, nor allow others to do so. Employee shall not alter or remove from the Confidential Information any copyright, trade secret, patent, or other proprietary legend, nor allow others to do so. Employee shall reproduce all proprietary notices on all copies Employee makes of the Confidential Information. Employee shall secure and protect the Confidential Information in a manner designed to prevent all access and uses thereof contrary to the terms of this Agreement. Employee further agrees that Employee shall use Employee's best efforts to assist the Company in identifying and preventing any use or disclosure of the Confidential Information contrary to this Agreement.

- Return of Company Confidential Information. Employee represents and warrants that, upon separation of employment, and without any request by the Company, Employee will return to Company any and all property, documents, and files (including all recorded media, such as papers, computer disks, copies, photographs, maps, transparencies, and microfiche) that contain Confidential Information or relate in any way to Company, the Affiliates or their business. Employee agrees, to the extent Employee possesses any files, data, or information relating in any way to Company, the Affiliates, or their business on any personal computer, Employee will delete those files, data, or information (and will retain no copies in any form). Employee also will return any Company tools, equipment, calling cards, credit cards, access cards or keys, any keys to any filing cabinets, vehicles, vehicle keys, and all other Company property in any form prior to the last date of employment.
- Injunctive Relief. In the event of a breach of any of the covenants in this Agreement, it is understood that damages will be difficult to ascertain and the Company and the Affiliates may petition a court of law or equity for injunctive relief in addition to any other relief which the Company and the Affiliates may have under the law or under this Agreement. It is hereby further agreed that the provisions of Section 1 and 2 are separate from and independent of the remainder of this Agreement and that these provisions are specifically enforceable by the Company notwithstanding any claim made by Employee against the Company.
- Intellectual Property. In consideration for employment with, or for continued employment with, the Company and for other good and valuable consideration, Employee agrees as follows:
  a. "Intellectual Property" means any and all original works of authorship, developments, concepts, improvements, designs, discoveries, ideas, trademarks, service marks, or trade secrets, or inventions, whether or not patentable or registrable under copyright or similar laws, which Employee may solely or jointly conceive or develop or reduce to practice, or cause to be conceived or developed or reduced to practice, during the performance of Employee's job duties for the Company.

b. Employee hereby assigns to the Company, or its designee, all of Employee's right, title, and interest in and to all Intellectual Property, except where prohibited by law, so that the Company is the exclusive owner of the Intellectual Property. Employee further acknowledges that all original works of authorship which are made by Employee (solely or jointly with others) within the scope of or during the performance of Employee's job duties for the Company and which are protectable by copyright are "works made for hire" as that term is defined in the United States Copyright Act, and that such works made for hire shall constitute part of the Intellectual Property. Employee understands and agrees that the decision whether or not to commercialize or market any Intellectual Property is within the Company's sole discretion and for the Company's sole benefit and that no royalty will be due to Employee as a result of the Company's efforts to commercialize or market any such Intellectual Property. Employee shall not use any Intellectual Property except for the exclusive benefit of the Company and the Affiliates.

c. Employee agrees to assist the Company, or its designee, at the Company's expense, in every proper way to secure or enforce the Company's rights in any Intellectual Property. In the event the Company is unable for any reason, after reasonable effort, to secure signature on behalf of Employee on any document needed for the actions specified in this Section, Employee hereby irrevocably designates and appoints the Company and its duly authorized officers and agents as Employee's agent and attorney-in-fact, which appointment is coupled with an interest, to act for and in Employee's behalf to execute, verify, and file any such documents, and to do all other lawfully permitted acts to further the purposes of this Section with the same legal force and effect as if executed by Employee. Employee hereby waives and quitclaims to the Company any and all claims, of any nature whatsoever, which Employee now or may hereafter have for infringement or misappropriation of any Intellectual Property assigned to the Company under this Agreement. Employee agrees to keep and maintain adequate and current records of all Intellectual Property made by Employee (solely or jointly with others) while employed by the Company. During the period Employee is employed by the Company, Employee shall promptly disclose to the Company fully and in writing all Intellectual Property authored, conceived or reduced to practice by Employee, either alone or jointly with others.

d. Employee has set forth in Exhibit A attached hereto a complete list of all inventions that Employee has, alone or jointly with others, conceived, developed, and reduced to practice prior to the commencement of Employee's employment with the Company, that Employee considers to be Employee's property or the property of third parties that Employee wishes to have excluded from the scope of this Agreement. Other than those items identified on Exhibit A, Employee warrants and represents that there are no original works of authorship, developments, concepts, improvements, designs, discoveries, ideas, trademarks, service marks, or trade secrets, or inventions which were made or acquired by Employee prior to Employee's employment by the Company, which are owned in whole or in part by Employee, which relate to the business, or the Company's proposed business, and which are not assigned to the Company under this Agreement.

- Non-Solicitation. During Employee's employment and for one (1) year immediately following termination of Employee's employment with the Company for any reason, whether with or without cause, Employee will not directly or indirectly solicit, entice, induce or attempt to induce or influence any employee, independent contractor, vendor, or supplier of the Company or the Affiliates to terminate or alter his, her, or its relationship with the Company or Affiliate.
- Business Opportunities. Employee shall promptly disclose to the Company all business ideas, prospects, proposals, and other opportunities pertaining to any aspect of the Company's or the Affiliates' business that are originated by any third parties and brought to the attention of Employee during the term of Employee's employment by the Company.
- Representations and Warranties. Employee hereby represents and warrants to the Company as follows:

a. Employee has full power, authority, and capacity to enter into this Agreement and to perform his obligations hereunder. This Agreement has been voluntarily executed by Employee and constitutes a valid and binding agreement of Employee;

b. Employee has read this Agreement and has had the opportunity to have this Agreement reviewed by Employee's legal counsel;

c. Given the nature of the business in which the Company and the Affiliates are engaged, the restrictions in Section 1 above are reasonable and necessary to protect the legitimate interests of the Company and the Affiliates;

d. Employee acknowledges and agrees that Employee's employment with, or continued employment with, the Company is sufficient consideration for this Agreement;
e. To the best of Employee's knowledge, Employee's employment with the Company will not (1) conflict with or result in a breach of any of the provisions of, (2) constitute a default under, (3) result in the violation of, (4) give any third party the right to terminate or to accelerate any obligation under, or (5) require any authorization, consent, approval, execution, or other action by or notice to any court or other governmental body under the provisions of any other agreement or instrument to which Employee is a party; and
f. Employee will notify business partners and future employers of Employee's obligations under this Agreement.

- At-Will Employment. Employee acknowledges that nothing in this Agreement, or any other policy or procedure at the Company, affects or alters Employee's at-will employment status at the Company. In other words, the Company may terminate Employee's employment at any time, for any reason or no reason, with or without warning, notice, or cause, just as Employee may terminate Employee's employment on the same basis.
- Assignment. Employee hereby acknowledges that this Agreement may not be transferred or assigned by Employee. The Company may transfer or assign this Agreement and its rights hereunder.
- Entire Agreement. This Agreement, including Exhibit A, is the entire agreement between the Parties concerning the subject matter of this Agreement. The Parties are not relying on any representations other than those set forth in this Agreement concerning the subject matter contained herein.
- Waiver and Modification. No waiver or modification of this Agreement or any covenant, condition, or limitation herein contained, shall be valid unless in writing and duly executed by Employee and the Company.
- Venue and Applicable Law. This Agreement shall be interpreted and construed in accordance with the laws of the State of *[YOUR STATE(S)]*, without regard to its conflicts of law provisions. Venue and jurisdiction will be in the *[YOUR STATE(S)]* state or federal courts.
- Severability. If any provision of this Agreement is held illegal, invalid, or unenforceable, such holding shall not affect any other provision hereof.

In the event any provision is held illegal, invalid, or unenforceable, such provision shall be limited so as to give effect to the intent of the Parties to the fullest extent permitted by applicable law.

- Survivorship. This Agreement shall be binding upon and inure to the benefit of the respective parties hereto and their executors, administrators, heirs, personal representatives, successors, and assigns.
- Counterparts. This Agreement may be executed in multiple counterparts, each of which shall be deemed an original, but all of which together shall constitute one and the same instrument.
- Attorneys' Fees. Employee agrees that if the Company prevails in any action or proceeding arising out of or relating to this Agreement, Employee shall pay the Company's reasonable costs and attorneys' fees incurred in such action or proceeding.

IN WITNESS WHEREOF, the Parties have executed this Confidentiality Agreement as of this ___ day of _____________, [YEAR].

[YOUR PRACTICE NAME]

| ___________________________ | ___________________________ |
|---|---|
| (signature) | By:<br>Title: |
| | ___________________________ |
| | (print name)<br>Exhibit A |

## Get Mobilized

You need to get moving toward your goal, swiftly, decisively, and with sound business tools. Doing this will enable you to make your new practice come alive and thrive.

I will provide you with tools to begin to articulate your dreams and goals about your new concierge medical practice. From those come the framework for the design of your new business model. Not the one that the media has been talking up or down, but your exclusive model. It doesn't have to be molded like some franchise practice of some big national concierge medicine chain. It has to feel comfortable and be your brand, not a subsidiary of Procter & Gamble.

We will explore what gets you excited about the practice of medicine—where your passion is. We'll explore how to describe your value proposition. We'll follow the steps to develop realistic, timed goals to achieve your objectives and turn our vision into reality for your private practice.

I will show you how to build a thriving practice without selling out to a franchise organization, without compromising your personal ethics, your brand image, or the love of medicine as a profession. In short order, you will see the change.

## Attributes of a Successful Concierge Physician

Since concierge medicine is essentially new as a trend, I will share a list of the attributes I've noticed in the most successful concierge medicine clients we've studied for market comparison and benchmarking, and those we've transitioned who have thrived.

1. They had specific, written goals, an action plan, and timelines by which they set deadlines to achieve them.
2. They articulate a feeling of entitlement to make money doing what they love to do.
3. They maintain a low-anxiety lifestyle. They don't live outside their means; they have a low debt-to-income ratio.
4. They are optimistic about their practice no matter what health-care reform throws at their colleagues who remain behind in traditional mainstream practices with managed care referral streams and Medicare madness.
5. They have a life, participate in the community, and enjoy time with family and friends.
6. They have a well-run practice that is professionally managed by a healthcare business specialist with training and education and experience that they can afford to attract and retain.
7. They are open to change, growth, and new service lines that bring revenue and add value to the practice, and that is meaningful to their patients.
8. Their membership fees are affordable to people of moderate means.
9. The have a written brand standard of operation that is characterized by integrity, kindness, compassion, and high ethical and customer service standards.

10. They exude confidence and control when you meet them in the practice, out in public, or at public events and speaking engagements to talk about their unique brand of healthcare.

Which of these traits describe you? To which do you aspire? They are all possible. So let's get started.

## Chapter 2

# Frequently Asked Questions

There are a few questions I am asked at almost every introductory phone call and initial consultation:

1. Am I ready to convert my practice?
2. How difficult will this be?
3. How long will it take?
4. How much will it cost?
5. Do I have to accept insurance and participate in managed care?
6. Do I have to forsake all the patients who won't pay the membership fee?
7. Can I set a fee and offer unlimited care in my practice each month in exchange for the fee?
8. Do I have to quit Medicare?
9. Do I have to be compliant with Health Insurance Portability and Accountability Act (HIPAA)?
10. Do I need an electronic medical records system?
11. Do I have to learn ICD-10?
12. Do I have to do social media and marketing?
13. Do I have to have a website?
14. Who can advise me how to get started?

So here are the answers:

1. It depends on your goals and objectives.
2. It depends on your level of preparation.
3. It depends on your level of commitment.

4. It depends on what you want or need to buy.
5. No.
6. No.
7. No.
8. No.
9. Most likely.
10. Probably.
11. Yes.
12. Yes.
13. Absolutely.
14. It depends on the kind of advice you are seeking. First, take with a grain of salt the quotes from unnamed and unproven "experts" and their vague, broad, and unexplained generalities. There are many out there. They are characterized as executive directors of such and thus, past presidents of this and that, bloggers, and marketing generalists who see concierge medicine as the next lucrative area of healthcare where the "frightened and frustrated" physicians (how's that for alliteration!) are aggregated as a new batch of customers with money.

## Evaluating the Advisors and Trends

If you haven't already figured it out, I am pretty direct. I say what I am thinking. I've been in the business for more than 30 years. My view is that concierge medicine is no more new than the concept of New Urbanism.* While the term *concierge medicine* may be a recently coined term or expression, applied as a conceptual business model for the private practice of medicine, the model itself is not new. What is new is charging a membership fee to entitle someone to the privileges associated with membership. It is present almost everywhere that a single-payer health insurance and social security system is in place around the world. It is new in the United States, but my perspective comes from my experience as an international healthcare business consultant. I've been working with doctors who have been operating a business model of *more personalized health delivery* for three decades. They are just now starting to market a package of amenities and membership privileges in exchange for a fee and a membership contract.

* New Urbanism website, http://www.newurbanism.org/newurbanism/principles.html.

Why did I compare it to New Urbanism? Because I am the group leader in my community's sustainable neighborhood Health and Wellness Task Force, and we are involved in a New Urbanism project in our neighborhood in trendy Northwest Denver. Urban planning and public health are closely related. But working on international development projects to bring modern healthcare to West Africa, imagine my surprise as I drove through the community streets in the town of Awka, Nigeria, in Anambra state, and saw the most rudimentary form of New Urbanism. It had all the elements, just not the fancy ultramodern buildings and upscale boutique shops to which I was accustomed. How new is that? Maybe *renewed* urbanism is what is happening in Northwest Denver, and *urbanism* is what people did in the 1920s and before when neighbors knew one another, people walked to streetcar stops, shopped locally, went to concerts at the gazebo in the park, lived with fewer modern conveniences and gizmos and gadgets, used less electricity, and grew gardens.

I also watch what is happening architecturally in this part of Denver with housing. People are buying 1920s Arts and Crafts era bungalows, bulldozing them, and reusing the land to build new single-family homes, duplexes, and triplexes. The interesting thing is that the design style of the new buildings all resemble "Walter Gropius wannabe Bauhaus design school" architecture complete with Ludwig Mies van der Rohe knock-off Barcelona chairs in every living room. The Barcelona chair, an icon of the modernist movement, exudes a simple elegance, epitomizing Mies's theory that less is more. It was popular in the 1920s—someplace else. I see the concierge medicine movement as very similar. Just as there are as many ways to design a home in the style of the Bauhaus design school that are reminiscent of Gropius, and filled with Barcelona chair replicas, so too are the many models based on this nebulous description of what defines concierge medicine. So the Bauhaus and modernist movement theme was "less is more," the theme of New Urbanism is essentially "sustainable placemaking," and the concierge medicine theme is "more personalized health delivery and healthcare comanagement by the doctor and the patient." As I see it, concierge medical practice design and business strategy is a matter of preference, design style, medical homemaking, sustainable healthful living, relationships, and packaging all that together to produce a product that is marketable to people who want to buy the concierge medicine amenities-based product coupled with the medical services they need. You could also say that it's tantamount to a house and furniture; the rest is design and architecture selected by the consumer on the basis of value and taste.

My experience, training, and personality influence my contempt for medical business advisors that exceed their scope of training and experience and market their consulting services and fallacy to physicians. Many of you are in need of a business advisor who will help you build a sound strategy from good guidance. You don't have money to spend on consultants in the first place, and you certainly don't have money to spend on fallacy, but you may not know fallacy when you see it. If you fall victim to these advisors, you risk building a strategy and business plan from that fallacy and poor guidance that can cause you to fail, and can cause you great expense to have to start over to rectify that which was done wrong, or based on fallacy, and doesn't get you to the objectives and goals you've established. Then again, business is risky. We all make the best business decisions we can, and as small business owners, we make choices—sometimes from instinct and hunches, other times from fact. Use every bit of critical thinking you can muster when vetting recommendations you read in blogs, books, and the media. Use logic when you interpret market research statistics and the training you have in understanding statistics: the sample size, the study participants, how they were selected, what was being studied, and how the results were reported.

For example, I've been fervently following the industry blogs and postings in LinkedIn on concierge medicine. I own three groups centered on concierge medicine and participate regularly in a fourth. There's also a lot of fallacy out there on concierge medicine transition readiness. For example, I've been poking around one blogger's website that states, "industry experts suggest …." The post has no attributions, explanations of research parameters, method or sample size, or just who these "experts" might be. A review of the blogger's background reveals that the blogger is a marketer. And quite adroit at search engine optimization (SEO) and search engine marketing (SEM). He's also quite clever in selling his self-published books and "research reports." He's found platforms to publish that require only a monthly fee for the privilege, and no real peer review. After so many posts and payments, one is labeled as an "expert author," and given a badge that can be superimposed on book covers and public profiles. The unsuspecting reader that encounters this blog might actually be convinced that these are all real certifications and credentials, until one digs deeper. The blogger is not a healthcare consultant, has never worked in healthcare business management or practice management. In this blogger's profile, there are glaring indications that the experience of the blogger is written up for the purpose of marketing. The blogger's courses cited don't include anything remotely related to managing a medical practice or having studied any courses on healthcare business administration topics, and the blogger has no clinical background. I guess what exasperated me the most was the post on the blog that suggested that in order to be considered *ready* to transition to concierge medicine, "a physician should have a minimum of 6 years in private practice" and that "10 years is preferable." My response to that is "Why?"

The only hypothesis I can raise is that at 10 years in practice, one might be far enough out from graduation and school debt and would be likely to have an established practice and at least a decent credit rating, and therefore might have enough money to pay the consulting fees charged by the blogger. Before reading these posts and pie-in-the-sky answers and giving them any importance, please do some critical thinking about the recommendations upon which you base strategy and take actions. Why 6? Why not 5 or 7? Why is 10 better? Before you believe all that you read for free on startup theory and strategy for concierge medicine, please consider the author's background. Your success and livelihood depend on it.

While I am on this subject, let's dig a little deeper into the flawed logic of this recommendation about having 6 to 10 years of experience. I call it a fallacy because it doesn't take into consideration all the issues and instances of a 6- to 10-year work history as a physician. It was a catchy title, about readiness to be a concierge physician. I assume that he does it for SEO value. There's nothing illegal about posting fallacy. He has a right to freedom of speech. For it to be bad faith, it would have to be that the author knows it is bad advice and posts it anyway. Chances are, this individual doesn't know any better. This blogger lacks the professional training and experience to know better. The blogger is selling what the blogger has available for sale. But wait, the blogger states, "Experts within the concierge medicine industry suggest that physicians (of any specialty) should have a minimum of 6 years in private medical practice. However, 10 or more years is preferable."

Who are these "experts" who agree with the blogger? In marketing, this is referred to as *bandwagon marketing*. Bandwagon marketing is a sales technique described as using consumer behavior to follow a trend that is created by the need or want of a mass populous. When the target consumer is swayed by a product or service, this creates a ripple effect, which in turn attracts new and unsuspecting potential consumers to desire the product as well. If the bandwagon effect is executed effectively, the *illusionary* trend seems accepted by a majority of people and others will join in. There's a lot of free advice out there on the Internet. That doesn't mean you should consider all that bloggers post about startup strategy and criteria for your new practice. But here's where I draw the line. These other illusionary experts to whom the bloggers refer are now in the same bucket with the blogger, supposedly supporting the blogger's fallacy.

I define *fallacy* as an incorrect argument in logic and rhetoric resulting in a lack of validity, or more generally, a lack of soundness. To the blogger's recommendation, I could ask, "What about the physician who has been in practice for 10 years as a hospitalist or an employee of a large practice?

In many instances, physicians with 6 to 10 years of experience often work under an employment agreement that prohibits them from announcing or otherwise circumventing the employer through a noncompete or anti-conversion provision.

When these physicians call us for advice about concierge medicine transition and startup, one reason we ask about their current situation is because this bit of knowledge regarding their current situation influences the strategy and the specific startup advice we offer. For starters, it is very likely that a physician in practice for 10 years might have a patient panel of 4,000 patients that have been treated or had an encounter with the physician or another member of the practice in the past 24 months. The conversion potential of those patients being converted is *zero*. The patient charts are off limits, and to use them or any of their associated personal health information (PHI), including the patients' contact information are off limits, and any use of them for the purpose of marketing to them about your impending transition to concierge medicine or private practice is tantamount to "theft and conversion" of property that is an asset of the employer. Will I help you get around that? Let me put it this way: Are you asking me to be an accomplice to a crime?

The doctor who has been an internist in a 14-doctor practice for 12 years but has that kind of provision in his or her contract is no better off than a doctor just starting out. Both are very different kinds of transitions or launch strategies. One has a potentially convertible base while the other one doesn't.

If, on the other hand, you have been a concierge physician for 3 to 5 years with one of the corporate-sponsored franchise models, you may also have to take the lab coat off and leave it with all the other branded belongings and start anew if you want to disassociate yourself with their brand and go off on your own in an independent concierge practice. Read the fine print in your contract. The experience won't be pleasant at 50-something and seeking an exit strategy.

Why does my consideration head in this direction? Because I am a specialist in this domain and authored the definitive *Handbook of Physician Employment Contracts* back in 1998, published in 1999, and now in its second edition. The first edition was copublished by the Medical Group Management Association and the Healthcare Financial Management Association, and was peer reviewed, not self-published, and offered for sale on Amazon.com. I bring that knowledge and wisdom with me when I consult on concierge medical practice transition. Does the consultant you've selected bring similar expertise and experience to his or her Internet blog articles, self-published e-books, LinkedIn discussions, and recommendations?

There are also consultants out there who are other concierge physicians; they converted their practice and are now concierge physicians consultants. So why are they consulting instead of practicing medicine? What are they selling? A case study?

## Learn How to Evaluate and Hire Professional Advice

If you are a buyer of consulting services, first learn how to buy and not be a victim of the *bandwagon effect* and become the object of a consulting firm's intention to sell the maximum number of hours or retainers to physicians considering transition or startup. Their purpose is to yield the most profits for their firm, not your practice. Their objective with that technique is to convince physicians that "everyone else" agrees with them and their advice. The technique is all about persuasion selling, which is the primary objective of this marketing strategy. It has nothing to do with what you want, what you need, or what's the best course of action for you to take.

# Chapter 3

# Turning Crisis into Opportunity

If you are reading this book, chances are high that you are at least considering entrepreneurship. In the exercises that await you in this book, you will work through several steps, among them, building a vision for your practice and developing the skills to get you there.

The rest of this book will provide insight, perspective, and how-to skills starting from suggested ways to critically evaluate what you find through Internet research, blogs, books, and the suggestions of well-meaning friends, family, acquaintances, and the media.

Immediately following Chapter 4, I will assign some pen-and-paper exercises starting with your ideal practice vision as an initial tool upon which other exercises will be built. In Chapter 4, I will try to persuade you to adopt my thinking about being flexible in your product design and strategy, and to evaluate opportunities, not all of which may apply to your specific situation.

You'll need to develop some business skills that you may already have, other skills, and concepts to which you may never have been previously exposed. You are a healing artist about to engage in the business of healthcare. Here is where the rubber meets the road. Most likely you were sent from the hallowed halls of your medical training without the complete set of necessary skills to earn a living to pay back your student loans. This is not impossible. You are intelligent, this is a requirement, you won't succeed without it. There is help available in the form of coaches, hired professionals (accountants, lawyers, and consultants), but you must choose wisely where you obtain competent counsel from others and how much you agree to pay for it.

You probably already know the gripping paralysis of fear. You must learn to think critically, and identify fallacy when you encounter it so you can compartmentalize it as such. If you don't take care with this, your strategy and all your assumptions and expenditures to support a flawed strategy that follows could be imperiled.

You will learn how to elegantly and ethically market your product and cast any preconceived notions or disdain for marketing to the side in favor of approaching marketing as education. Promotion and advertising is very different from marketing. I will cover the differences and how branding, advertising, marketing, promotion, and public relations all fit together. Your job will be to take that training and decide how to use it in a way that feels natural and honest to you.

All businesses, whether they are a medical practice or a shoe store or a hamburger stand, have a common thread that includes a purpose, structure, needs, and goals. If you are a reader who is a physician based in the United States, many things that you may want to do in your private practice may make business sense in a capitalist society but may be illegal because there may be regulatory constraints that prohibit you from making certain offers or selling certain services to groups of individuals or advertising in a particular way. The same offer in Spain or Colombia or Dubai, India, South Africa, Australia, or Peru may be totally permissible and within the law.

# Chapter 4

# Determining If You Are Ready to Enter Concierge Medicine

When we are asked our opinion about a physician's readiness to enter concierge medicine, as you can see by what I wrote previously, there is no key performance indicator (KPI) or benchmark simply dictated by the number of years you've been in practice. To assume there is, is tantamount to assuming there is only one way to convert or launch a concierge medical practice. If you find otherwise, please call me toll free, at 800-727-4160 and point it out to me.

I believe that readiness for concierge medicine is determined on the basis of many indicators. The number of years in practice should be one of the lowest items on the list of criteria or concerns. After all, the number of years in practice is not something you can easily change, so while it has some importance, there are other indicators with higher priority—the first of which is having a solid brand, a favorable image in the community, being established in a market where many people can afford to buy a $5 coffee each morning at a coffee shop, and where the market has begun showing signs of increasing difficulty obtaining a primary care appointment within 3 days of a request for routine follow-up and within 5 days of a new patient visit, for starters.

## Financial Readiness

I consider your readiness to open a concierge practice within a composite framework. First, you will need to have a financial cushion to sustain you through the startup or rebranding period (not by how much you can spend on the consulting services). This does not mean I expect you to have a big pile of cash on hand. I consider financial readiness as follows:

- no bad debt lurking in the shadows
- a 700+ credit rating
- no active lawsuits or regulatory compliance risk exposures
- no criminal background, and a clean unrestricted license to practice medicine
- school loans, home, and business bills all currently paid as due
- a 6-month cash cushion in the bank for your personal expenses
- a steady income stream and a business line of credit available of up to $250,000 dollars
- you are in average good health and emotionally ready to take on additional stressors
- if married or in a relationship, that the relationship is stable and thriving

If you don't currently meet all those criteria, then how close do you come?

## Strategic Readiness

When evaluating your readiness to convert or launch a concierge medical practice, we consider your strategy and the market suitability for this business model where you intend to situate the practice.

We analyze the competition around you—both known and those competitors yet to be revealed, and the threat they pose to your ability to attract adequate market share. We also consider the concierge membership product you plan to offer to the market, the market's perceived need for your concierge membership product, its value proposition, the market's ability to afford your concierge membership product, and the market's level of sophistication to understand your concierge membership product. If the readiness is not clear, then something has to change.

In Douglas E. Goldstein's *Alliances: Strategies for Building Integrated Delivery Systems* (1995, Jones & Bartlett) the author discussed the various approaches to building integrated health delivery systems. He recommended matching the model to the market (MMM) as a late-stage approach toward successful integrated health delivery system strategies. This is relevant to the strategy for building a concierge medical practice as well. If you build a concierge medical practice design strategy that doesn't fit the market in which you will establish the practice, it matters not how many years you have in practice. The practice strategy will ultimately fail. It is far easier to change your strategy than it is to change or "disrupt" the market.

In your concierge medical practice strategy, you are not looking to change the world, or change the market. You are looking for 300–600 individuals who are willing to purchase what you have on offer. Once you hit your target, your strategy has to have a sustainability plan to maintain those members so that they renew, or are replenished if some leave. Beyond that, you have to either add a new practitioner, or put interested purchasers on a waiting list for an opening when there is a capacity to bring them in. It is far easier to adjust your strategy before implementation than after, so your readiness is measured also in terms of flexibility in your approach, the match of your model to your market. If you are not willing to adjust your strategy and your business model, you probably aren't ready to enter concierge medicine with an expectation that your new practice will thrive.

## Your Current Brand Reputation

We also take into consideration consumer behavior and your brand's reputation in your chosen market. Do consumers in the neighborhood actively post their ratings on social media channels such as Yelp, Google+, and other social media sites? Do they post ratings on HealthGrades.com, ZocDoc.com? If yes, what has the market said about your current brand, if you have one?

If we go back to my issues with the blogger's 6- to 10-year unsubstantiated recommendation for a moment, there are effective ways to convert or start concierge medical practices in a market—regardless of the past work history and practice setting. But a doctor who has been in practice and disgruntled for 10 years may have horrible social media rankings and comments out there that will be difficult to erase or bury—especially if the complaints are unanswered, and have merit. If this is your situation, we may suggest you completely rebrand your practice, or relocate if you want to or have to start anew. The nature of the posts about your brand will tell us if it was your personality, your staff's personality, an unreasonable expectation, a recurring problem, or something else that is doing well or broken and how easy or challenging it will be to rehabilitate.

## Will You Be Converting an Existing Practice?

When we evaluate a practice for transition, we ask how many active patients you have under your care. We define *active patients* as those that have visited you in the office in the past 24 months. The blogger in the previous chapter asserts that his research indicates you "should have a patient panel of at least 1800." Here, the blogger gives this authoritative statistic as a result of "research." The result of the research is published with no sample size or other panel information. Again I ask, "Why that number?" They also make a recommendation that you "have a minimum of 15 patients per day or an average of 60 patients per week prior to making a transition into concierge medicine." Again, I find myself asking, "Why that number?"

A minimum of 15 patients per day means what exactly? It has no bearing on the real revenues and relative value units being rendered each day. That can only be determined after one takes into consideration the evaluation and management level of service of those visits, the charges generated by the evaluation and management services, the contracted reimbursement rates of those visits, the denials and properly paid claims ratios, and collections of copayments and deductibles success. But what of the ancillary services for procedures? Ancillary services offered in a practice change the revenue potential of the practice drastically. Are the medical assistants you employ cost centers or revenue generators? How physicians practice—the number of patients they see, the hours they work, the type of insurance they accept—has a direct impact on patient access to medical services. So to make recommendations about specific numbers and volumes without any qualifiers, and without any explanation of the research conducted and its conclusions could cause a doctor considering a concierge medicine startup or transition to be influenced by another fallacy.

In results from a 2012 publication, *A Survey of America's Physicians* by the Physicians Foundation, over 59% of physicians surveyed in 2012 said they see 20 patients or fewer per day, up from 39.11% in 2008. The average number of patients seen per day by physicians in 2012 was 20.01, down from 23.43 in 2008, a decline of 16.6%.*

* This report summarizes the results of one of the largest and most comprehensive physician surveys ever undertaken in the United States. The survey was sent by email to over 630,000 physicians (approximately 84% of all physicians in active patient care), or to virtually every physician with an email address on file with the nation's largest physician database. The report includes responses from 13,575 physicians. Physicians Foundation, March 8, 2014, page 45, http://www.physiciansfoundation.org/uploads/default/Physicians_Foundation_2012_Biennial_Survey.pdf .

The patient volume per day is also dictated by the status of the physician. Employed physicians are often reported to be less motivated than self-employed physicians, so inferences about practices and the numbers of patients being seen in a day and the size of a patient panel are not clear KPIs upon which we make decisions about conversion readiness.

Be advised. Some consultants use this data to infer assumptions about your current revenues and expenses. They will then use conjecture to assume overheads by using crude assumptions and other bloggers' market guides to try to figure out what's left in your wallet—and take it from you. If you are asked these questions, you must consider what they will do with the information. Back-of-the-envelope math should never be used to build strategy; it should be used to wipe up spills. Don't get sold on a big bill or retainer as a result of the conjecture associated with it.

If you are already in practice, we take into consideration the demographic profile and socioeconomic and education profile of your patients. Concierge medicine annual membership fees range all across the board and include all kinds of packaged amenities and medical services for the money paid. Without considering the inclusions, there is no way to determine if the price is set properly.

Currently, since there is no official registry and no official definition of what constitutes a concierge medicine practice, there is no way to accurately measure how many concierge medical practices are in business and how many are in the prelaunch planning stages. As a result, there is also no way to accurately determine their business models, or their price point. But the truth of it all is that it doesn't really matter. That's like saying, "Maria, I want a steak for dinner tonight." Do we care how many steaks there are in the United States just waiting to be cooked? Or what cuts of meat are represented? Or what they all cost? Nope. We only care about the one we will choose from the butcher where we buy steaks, and which one we are going to select to sear on the grill. The rest are all steaks without much consequence in the grand scheme of things.

Since there is no active and objective registry or any unbiased and ongoing survey, that bit of data doesn't really matter. There is no such credible generally available data. The data for your particular situation must be created just for your instance. When an experienced consultant assesses your readiness to enter concierge medicine, the consultant must evaluate the specifics of the market around you and the demographics and socioeconomic status of the target communities within a drivable distance of 20–25 minutes. What the consultant does with that data during the interpretation of the data and the determination of its relevance to your particular strategy is where the value of the advice is measured. This is something we do when we come on site for our first visit with a client. It is included in the price of the first visit. It doesn't have to cost tens of thousands of dollars, but my approach to this is vastly different from most other consultants.

I subcontracted my services as a healthcare consultant for several years to Maritz Research, one of the largest custom market research companies in the United States and among the top 15 research companies in the world. That's where I get my market research and analysis skills and experience. It's how I learned how to size up a market, a competitor, and analyze the competition, and it subliminally influences what I do with the information I gather to make unique, custom suggestions for clients. I don't just pull ideas for you out of thin air, and they are not the same ideas for you as they would be for someone else. They may seem automatic and without effort, but when I analyze data, create worksheets, checklists, and other materials, these all come from my unique experiences. In the hands of another user, it is highly likely that the tools will be used differently and that the analysis of the data and its transformation into useful information will produce different results because of their different perspectives.

## Your Resources and Assets

Sometimes new practices "inherit" space from someone that is free or low rent, and other times they haven't yet signed a lease. Either way, there are solutions or workarounds so don't get all stressed out over the demographics, socioeconomic status, and education numbers. They have a place in the assessment, but there are no hard and fast rules or benchmarks here. The same goes for age ranges and gender distributions.

Back to the bandwagon blogger's suggestions. The blogger asserts, "According to [unnamed] industry consultants, more than 50% of your current patient-base (last 24 months) should be 40+ in order to start, sustain and grow a successful concierge medicine practice in the future." My same question applies, "Why that number and that age grouping?" There is no hard data to support such fallacy. So what does it say about the consultants upon whom that blogger relies?

You can start a concierge practice with no existing patients, and no specific age group. What is more important than a certain percentage of your patient base grouped into an age-band, or gender, or something else, is designing a viable concierge membership product that the market finds valuable and is willing to pay money for. You don't need 1,800, you need 300–600 patients.

Consider this: If you wait until you have 1,800 to 4,000 active patients to be ready to convert, how many disgruntled people will you jettison if you don't make provisions to care for them outside your concierge practice? And if you have business asset value in the ongoing business with the 1,800–4,000 and you send them all away if they won't buy a membership, are you tossing away that value and sending them to your competitors with a big red bow around their heads? Are you inviting them to post negative ratings on social media sites because of the disruption in the doctor–patient relationship and feeling of abandonment? How silly is that?

Readiness for concierge medicine entry or transition is a strategic determination. It is very personal, and its determining factors are based on unique circumstances relevant to your individual plan, product design, personality, and personal and business circumstances. No free self-test of four or five questions on someone's blog will ever do your situation justice. If you make business decisions based on a free blog you find from an author that has exceeded his or her scope of expertise and just wants to sell consulting and books as a means of income, I wish you all the best of luck. You will need more than luck, but that's a start. Please study up and get qualified advice no matter whom you hire.

## Exercise 1: Setting the Vision for Your New Practice

Get a piece of paper and a pencil with an eraser, not a pen. You may find you want to restate things and a pen will make things messy. Close your eyes and relax. Imagine your ideal concierge medical practice. How does it look and feel?

Now give yourself permission to imagine what you would like to create. Don't permit yourself to be distracted by frustrations or fears about money, managed care, Medicare, school debt, or what people have said about concierge medical practices and membership sales. For a few moments in time, everything is excellent.

First, write down why you decided to become a physician. Become introspective.

Fast forward 5 years into the future. Your practice can be anything you want it to be. You are enjoying your work as a concierge physician. Your practice has grown and developed and your membership capacity is at the maximum that you targeted. You find going to work each day intellectually stimulating, fun, and rewarding in a variety of ways. See it, hear it, experience it. Your ideal practice of the future.

Next, write down the answers to these questions:

1. What is it about your practice in the 5-year future that you enjoy the most?
2. What does your office look and feel like?
3. Describe your concierge members.
4. What are your work hours?
5. How many patients do you see in a day?
6. On average, how long do you spend with each patient for a routine office visit?
7. How much money do you make each month in revenue?
8. How much is your take-home pay?
9. What percentage of your patients are managed care?
10. What percentage of your patients are covered by Medicare?
11. What is your lifestyle like?
12. How much of your life is centered around family?
13. Where do you go for vacations? How often?
14. What do you do for fun each week?

Now let's come back to the present.

1. How would you feel if you achieved all of these goals?
2. What changes would have to take place to make all this happen?
3. Are you willing to do all that it will take to achieve your vision?

Congratulations! You just wrote the most primitive blueprint for your new concierge medicine practice and your business goals. The last two questions are the most important ones. If you are willing to make a strong commitment to work hard at all the incremental steps to build your practice, you can achieve your goals. Be prepared to hit a few bumps along the way, to encounter fear or failure a few times, get past the daily inertia, or doing things that you may at first find unfamiliar or uncomfortable and outside your comfort zone. With practice, if you are willing to do what it takes, you may be surprised that the transition or launch was not as difficult as you may have imagined.

Stretching past your comfort zone is something you did during your training the first time you intubated someone, or the first time you used a scalpel on a living breathing patient, or the first time you drew a blood sample or gave an injection. You had to get past that to get to where you are now. It is a normal part of the identity transition from the mainstream business model practice to concierge medical business and owning the reality that you are also a business owner and an entrepreneur, which involves risk.

## Exercise 2: Determining Your Comfort with Business Ownership

Small business ownership takes guts to get started and succeed. Some of the traits and life experiences you have encountered up until now have contributed to your comfort or angst with business ownership. If you've never owned and operated a business before, there are some things to think about before you decide if you are ready to bet on yourself.

Take this short quiz and let's see where the subtle influences pop up. (The numbers In parentheses are points attributable to each answer.)

1. In what kind of employment setting did your parents work?
   - A. Both worked and were self-employed for most of their working lives (10).
   - B. Both worked and were self-employed for some part of their working lives (5).
   - C. One parent was self-employed (5).
   - D. Neither parent was self-employed (2).
2. Have you ever been fired from a job?
   - A. Yes, more than once (5).
   - B. Yes, once (4).
   - C. No (3).
3. Are you an immigrant or were your parents or grandparents immigrants?
   - A. I was born outside the country in which I presently reside (5).
   - B. One or both of my parents were born outside the country where I presently reside (4).
   - C. At least one of my grandparents was born outside the country in which I presently reside (3).
   - D. Does not apply (0).

4. Your professional career has been:
   A. Primarily in small businesses (fewer than 100 employees) (10).
   B. Primarily in medium-sized businesses (100–500 employees) (5).
   C. Primarily in big businesses (over 500 employees) (0).
5. Did you operate any businesses before the age of 20?
   A. Many (10)
   B. Few (7)
   C. None (0)
6. What is your present age?
   A. 28–30 (8)
   B. 31–40 (10)
   C. 41–50 (5)
   D. Over 50 (2)
7. What would be your primary motivation for starting a business of your own?
   A. To make more money (0).
   B. I don't like working for someone else (15).
   C. To be famous (0).
   D. As a means to have clinical autonomy (10).
8. What is/was your relationship to the parent who provided most of the family's income?
   A. Strained (10)
   B. Comfortable (5)
   C. Competitive (10)
   D. Nonexistent (5)
9. You arrive at answers to difficult questions by:
   A. Working hard (0)
   B. Working smart (5)
   C. Both (10)
10. If you were at the horse races, which of these would you bet on?
   A. The daily double (0)
   B. A 10–1 shot (2)
   C. A 3–1 shot (10)
   D. A 2–1 favorite (3)
11. The only ingredient that is both necessary and sufficient for starting a business is:
   A. Money (0)
   B. Customers (10)

C. An idea or product (0)
D. A combination of motivation and hard work (0)

Let's analyze your answers.

Score—your entrepreneurial profile:

| | |
|---|---|
| 125–115 | You will probably be successful as an entrepreneur. |
| 115–124 | Entrepreneur |
| 105–114 | Underlying entrepreneur |
| 95–104 | Potential entrepreneur |
| 85–94 | Borderline entrepreneur |
| Below 84 | Employee physician |

If you scored below 115, don't despair. The test is used to screen for traditional entrepreneurs, and physicians have a strong mindset for entrepreneurship. What it tells you is that you may have to stretch a little further and understand what attracts you to concierge medicine as a business model.

# Chapter 5

# What Sets You Apart from Other Concierge Physicians?

Many concierge physicians consider themselves primary care physicians. They practice a great deal of family medicine and internal medicine for adults. They treat individuals, families, and couples. Yet what sets one physician apart from the others are the special professional interests they enjoy as well as their unique knowledge and training in certain clinical areas.

Many of the concierge physicians I've been hired to advise are very open to learning new things, adding new procedures, and making new services available to their patients. Several have expanded traditional primary care service lines to include aesthetics and anti-aging, nutrition, stem cell therapies, and plasma-rich platelet (PRP) therapies, while others have affiliated with a part-time therapist to provide addiction counseling, family therapy, executive coaching and stress management, and travel medicine and immunizations, especially where the only other alternative is the pharmacy on the corner or the health department. Still others have added acupuncture and alternative and complementary medicine services such as massage, personal training, and more.

For example, my concierge physician does a better job at trigger point injections than any orthopedic surgeon or physiatrist I've ever met. I was really nervous the first time, but I figured, "I am a big girl, my knee hurts, I can take it." I. He was less expensive and it was easier to get an appointment, and I was able to proceed with my duties as a speaker and make my rounds on hospital inspections in three countries on my impending whirlwind tour around Greece, Turkey, and the Ukraine.

But primary care physicians are not the only ones that enter concierge medicine. In recent months, the concierge medicine business model has piqued the curiosity of many specialists. Specialists are also among the fearful and frustrated, and for some patients with complex chronic diseases, concierge specialty care may be the most effective treatment approach.

Regardless of your ilk and training, you need to view yourself as a specialist of something. The advantage you have with a medical license is that you can design a practice in a concierge business model that can last for decades without getting bored. You can evolve your practice into a niche within a specialty without having to change careers. Your specialty interests can parallel your own interests, social trends and needs, and areas of medicine that touch you personally.

As you develop expertise in a specialty, you become really adroit in your niche and you can design your practice to capture the essential elements to brand your niche in medicine, if only in your town or region. With this liberation and permission to choose, you will rediscover the delight in the practice of medicine, do it well,and attract more patients who see the passion, and more referrals from your colleagues who can discern your engagement and enthusiasm to do your best for their patients. They in turn will send you more referrals because the experience for the patient and the referring physician will be mutually beneficial. When they refer a patient to you and the patient is happy with the encounter, it is an excellent reflection on the referring physician.

You will also be in an excellent position to reach out to those referring physicians and inform them about your special interests and educate them about the value of concierge medicine as a business model.

## How to Describe Your New Business Model

The public needs to understand what you do and how you can help them. Telling people that you are a physician with a concierge medicine practice is so nonspecific that it doesn't tell them what you do and how they might benefit from joining your practice. If someone is sitting next to you, and asks what you do, you might try some of these explanations:

> *I am a primary care physician with a private practice. I specialize in [...] and I have a special interest in [...].*

> *I conduct clinical trials on stem cells to see if we can safely and effectively treat [...] disease/condition better than we currently do for patients.*

When you phrase it this way, you are inviting them into a conversation. You can talk about wellness, prevention, disease avoidance, and how having a more accessible relationship with their physician is beneficial and can actually save money on healthcare. Then, if the person asks how to get in touch with you to learn more, or wants to follow your blog, or visit your website for some handy tip sheets, you can give her your card.

Sometimes, those encounters lead to invitations for speaking engagements and other public relations opportunities. Sometimes, they lead to a new subscriber to your blog or a membership purchase in your practice.

When you tell people that your specialty involves working with (not treating) people (not patients) who have a certain chronic condition, you also provide an opportunity to educate them if they are interested. If not, they will let you know by their reaction. Watch for the cues and the body language.

Developing an approach that puts you in a position as an authority on something, and categorizes you as a specialist in a niche within medicine is good for your public image, good for your practice, and good for the public, because it gives you a chance to educate and spread good information. Learn to talk in "people terms" about your work and how much you enjoy it.

## Developing a Market Niche within Your Specialty

Developing a market niche doesn't require board certification and fellowship. It is defined by consumer need and preferences regarding services they find valuable and for which they are willing to pay money.

The typical consumer persona who purchases a concierge membership is one that is likely to seek out a specialist of whatever health concerns they have, if they can find one. In order for them to find you, you have to market and promote your niche effectively. If you don't know how to do this, find a consultant that can help you and teach you what to say, where to promote it, and how to describe the niche you've chosen.

In order to decide on an area of specialization and turn it into a market niche, don't limit your consideration to your formal training and clinical experience. Your goal is to connect with about 300–600 people who reside within a drivable distance to your practice and convert them into concierge members. The way to connect the market niche to the market is with a solid, integrated marketing strategy and implementation plan to execute the strategy. This holds true whether you are a primary care physician or a neurologist or rheumatologist.

While this is something we can do for you as consultants, you can do it yourself. It isn't difficult. To begin, first survey the needs of your community. This is part of your market assessment and analysis. A niche is like a slot—in this case, an unfilled one, for which there is a market need.

## Exercise 1: Market Niche Data Collection

Get a pen and paper. Answer the following questions and place your findings in a three-ring binder under a tab labeled "Market Research."

Answer the following questions:

1. In your practice, how many active (seen in the last 24 months) patients do you have?
2. Sort them by zip codes. Download the list as a spreadsheet file.
3. Enter the zip codes in the zip code map lookup at http://www.usnaviguide.com/zip.htm.
4. Download all the maps you create so you have a visual picture of the distance your patients travel to come to you. This is your catchment area, the area and population from which your business currently attracts visitors or customers. This map will tell you the population for each zip code in your catchment area. Record that in the column to the right of the number of times the zip code occurs on your spreadsheet. Title that column "Homes." This will help you visualize your market size.
5. Next, if you are already established in a traditional practice, run a report from your practice management software that identifies the ICD-9 codes you have recorded and list them by highest to lowest frequency. If you have the option, list the description in words, next to the numeric code.
6. Next, run a report that counts the patients in your practice by the year of their birth. Tally those into logical groupings of 5- to 10-year increments.
7. If your software offers the chance to identify patients that speak a particular language, download that report as well, by age and/or by zip code. (If you can get both, great!)

8. Determine how many children, seniors, and people from other cultures or representatives of significant groups are currently patients of your practice. See if you can find out from the city or county what percentage of total population these groups represent, correlating numbers for your catchment area as a whole. Then determine how much market share you have of each, by percentage. This information will likely help you identify any unique market niches or medically underserved populations.
9. Obtain a list of licensed physicians in your catchment area from the board of professional regulation in your catchment area jurisdiction(s). If you live near a state border (like Four Corners, New Mexico, for example) you may need to gather data from more than one jurisdiction. If possible, sort the list by registered specialty. Pay particular attention to those who specialize in the same or similar market niches to those in which you have an interest to develop further into an area of specialization. This will help you prioritize your choices a little better.
10. You can also perform similar research on the businesses in your area. Is there a market niche in executive checkups, travel medicine, people who sit all day, people who stand all day, people who fly for their work or some other significant activity, such as people who work with certain elements or chemicals (miners, coal workers, heavy metals and toxins, etc.)? Make notes on those bits of information. One source of this information may actually be your public health department.
11. Contact the office of economic development for your catchment area. Find out if people are moving into the area or out of the area, and any demographic information you can gather about the move-ins. Also, if available, find out the average income of the people in your catchment area. This is usually available from U.S. Census data. You can also access it by searching for "Average Income by Zip Code" in Google.

Now that you've done the research and gathered the data, you have to analyze it in context. This is where you may need professional help. If we were doing this research in our office, we would have had a research assistant or a geographic information system (GIS) intern do the data gathering, but the analysis takes professional insight and experience to know what to do with it.

You may already have the skills to think creatively about how to build your practice, and your mind will easily turn ideas into specialties and specialties into market niches. If you are unclear how to process this data into useful information, ask for assistance.

Here are some ideas you can start with:

- High-profile and prominent people in your community
- People who may want to maintain the strictest level of confidentiality such as sports figures, newscasters, politicians, prominent business leaders, entertainers, and so on
- People who may not want to be on an electronic medical record ("preppers" and survivalists)
- Wealthy people who demand a certain class of service
- People who engage in certain sports activities
- People with infertility problems, cardiac problems, neurological problems, psychiatric problems, trauma victims, AIDS/HIV patients, patients with autoimmune diseases, patients with lung diseases, cancer patients, patients interested in clinical trials, etc.
- Your creativity goes here: what else?

## Exercise 2: Choosing Your Market Niche

Now it is time to focus on the specialties that interest you enough to be considered as a market niche for you. In Exercise 1, you produced your ideal practice vision. Whatever you decide here has to be integrated into that vision statement or aligned with it. It is okay to change the vision, but document why you changed it and something to jar your memory about your thinking as you processed the information, gained new insight, or were influenced by something specific.

1. Start by listing the potential areas of specialization.
2. Add new specialties as you think of them.
3. Cross out the ones that no longer match your vision or strategy.
4. What's left? Write down any notes about each one that inspires you. We will use this in creating your living brand in future exercises.
5. What issues or clinical populations are on your list for which you have the most passion? List the reasons next to the items on your list.
6. What do you know intuitively and enjoy the most about your specialty?
7. What topics did you pursue during your fellowship, if you did one?
8. In what area is your community medically underserved?
9. With what diagnoses or groups of patients have you done most of your work?

10. With what diagnoses or groups of patients have you derived the most gratification?
11. Which diagnoses or groups of patients would you like to grow to a larger percentage of your practice? Why?
12. With what specialties might you use your natural talents, hobbies, and interests?
13. Are there any transference or counter-transference concerns that arise in any of these potential niches? If so, can you resolve them ethically or otherwise manage them?
14. Which specialties may be oversupplied by clinicians? Are there enough patients to sustain your new concierge practice? Remember, your goal is only 300–600 subscribing members.
15. Are there sources of referrals to connect with these market niche prospects? List as many referral sources, community groups, and agencies or organizations as you can for each niche specialty. (Think public relations opportunities here!)
16. Which specialties are not as dependent on managed care (consider this if you plan to reduce your managed care participation)?
17. Can you achieve the income level you want to earn with the specialties you have listed?
18. Which specialties will allow you to live the lifestyle you would like to live? (No late calls, longer vacation potential with remote access, etc.)
19. Will you need any additional training to master competence in this area? How will you obtain that training, and from whom? Will you need to attend continuing medical education (CME)? How much will it cost and how long will it take? Are you willing to put in the required time and investment?
20. How will you describe yourself as a community expert in your chosen special niche? (Write down your opening statement using the skills you learned in Chapter 5.)
21. How does each of these choices fit into your practice vision and long-term goals?
22. Which specialty niche is your best choice if you had to start tomorrow?
23. Are you willing to commit whatever it takes to build a thriving concierge practice in this market niche?

Researching your niche will take time. You should set aside several hours to fill in any gaps in your knowledge, read abstracts, books, and other relevant information and data to build your competence in your market niche.

Concierge medicine is highly geared to personalized convenience for patients. That includes saving them time on Internet research by having materials and reports and data and articles they can find easily using your website instead of the *universe* of Google. Build a bibliography as this may also make good content for articles you write for your blog or reference materials you want to have on hand on your concierge practice website.

Now that you've done these exercises and a little introspection, it is time to start working on designing the practice and planning strategies and action plans.

## Turning Your Chosen Market Niche into Something Marketable

Once you've decided on a passion or interest that you want to claim as your niche, you must become the leading authority on that market niche by demonstrating *expert power.*

True market leadership in a niche comes from expert power. This may not actually be as far from your comfort zone as you might believe. Let me explain. There are two things that are known about leadership:

1. Leadership is about much more than being responsible for other people.
2. Leadership, and more importantly market leadership, is a role that you can choose.

This means that you can be a leader in your own way, whether you're currently in a formal leadership role or not.

Having responsibility for people and projects does not automatically make you a leader. Leadership is more of a process than a position: it's a process of identifying what needs to be done, knowing how to influence others to achieve this goal, making sure that the job is done well, and building an even stronger team.

There are four key sources of formal power:

- **Legitimate power**—power that comes with a particular position or title
- **Reward power**—power from the authority to give rewards
- **Coercive power**—power from the authority to punish
- **Information**—power from exclusive access to information

You will be exercising formal power in several ways. As the owner of the practice, you immediately assume three of the four formal powers (power to rule, reward, or punish). You can reward employees, discipline and punish employees, and set the rules of business. You will also have the formal power over vendors and suppliers. The fourth source of power is one you have but not all physicians elect to use it. This is the power to teach others and share the information they have. The teaching is not only limited to employees, but extends to the community at large, your patients, nurses at the hospital, technicians that perform procedures or diagnostic testing, and more.

While it's true that many people in authority may possess these sources of power, it's not enough to make them leaders. These are not inspirational or motivational sources of power; therefore, the power is unlikely to be permanent. There may also be negative consequences if the power is used incorrectly or inappropriately.

Think about people you've worked with whose leadership was based on formal power alone (in other words, not based on charisma, expertise, or setting a great personal example—we'll look at these later). Write their names in Table 5.1.

Next, determine what type of formal power they held. Were they leaders because they were the bosses? Did they lead by intimidation or coercion? Think of at least one person for each base of power. If you can't think of an example from your own life, think of a general group of people who might use that source of power. (For example, the popular doctors or surgeons

**Table 5.1 Effective Use of Formal Powers**

| *Person* | *Base of Power* | *Effectiveness* |
|---|---|---|
| Chief of Staff | | |
| Your Spouse | | |
| | | |
| | | |
| | | |
| | | |
| | | |
| | | |

at the hospital could be seen as leaders because they have the power to reward others with inclusion in their group.)

Last, analyze the long-term effectiveness of each person's power. How likely is it that people continued to follow this person, even as circumstances changed?

After finishing this exercise, it should be clear that formal power is not necessarily effective for true leaders—these are the leaders you want to please, who inspire you to work hard, and who have made a real difference in your life. These people are likely to derive most of their power from informal sources. Of course, they may also have formal power in terms of title and ability to reward, but these are not their only bases of power.

In addition to the four sources of formal power, there are three sources of informal power:

- **Charismatic power—**power that comes from a person's natural charm and charisma. (You and your team must demonstrate charisma to be able to seem affable and approachable, or people won't buy a membership in your practice.)
- **Referent power—**power from treating people well, setting a good example, demonstrating integrity, and generally behaving in such a way that others seek to please the leader and emulate their behavior. (They need to see you in the community doing healthful things, exercising, eating right, and taking care of your own health.)
- **Expert power—**power from having employees, other health professionals and allied health technicians, the public at large, and already established patients with whom you've developed a relationship know and believe that their leader has the knowledge, skills, and experience to lead them.

These informal sources of power are the most compelling. Charisma is often a natural trait that people possess—it's quite difficult to learn to be charismatic (although it is possible). On the other hand, you can learn and develop expert and referential power much more easily. With these two power bases, you have the foundation for becoming a *transformational* leader—a leader who has integrity, inspires people with a shared vision of the future for their good health and well-being, one how sets clear goals for them, and one who motivates people toward those goals and communicates well.

To become an influential market leader as a concierge physician, you must not only wield the power, you must make people feel good as a result of your leadership. But having it is not the same as mastering how to use it to set you apart in the market niche you've chosen.

In a leadership role, your patients and employees and others with whom you enjoy professional relationships will look to you for direction and support. They need to believe that you know what you're doing, and that you have the ability to guide them to success. This is why having expert power is so important if you want to be a good concierge physician and a healthcare leader.

When you're perceived as an expert, people trust you. For example, physicians trust consultants to help them build a practice, guide strategic planning, keep them in compliance with regulations, and execute strategies or troubleshoot problems in their practice, because of their expertise. This is the same sort of trust that your team members give you when you're the expert.

Along with trust in your skills comes trust in your judgment. As an expert, patients and other healthcare professionals in the community will bring problems that they're having, and trust that you will know how to produce excellent results. They will also trust that you have the wisdom needed to reach the end goal or objective they want to achieve. All of this will lead your followers to respect you and your abilities as a concierge physician within your chosen market niche.

As a whole, expert power helps you influence people's behavior, and motivate them to do great things. Because you will earn the respect of your followers and your peers, you will likely have fewer of the people problems that nonexpert leaders have.

## Building the Expertise in Your Market Niche

By definition, an expert has specialized skill and ability. As an expert in concierge medical business development, I know what I am doing, what needs to be done, and how to guide doctors and their managers on what needs to be done to secure a positive outcome. But I am not an expert in everything. So, to be a leader with expert power, I had to identify what I am an expert in, what I needed to become expert in, and what I wanted to become an expert in. I also needed to know what I don't know, so that I could bring in other experts when I need them. This is also true for you.

Expert power starts with an inventory of one's current skills and expertise. In Table 5.2, the goal of the exercise is to identify the leadership roles in which you will be the most successful.

**Table 5.2 Identifying Your Areas of Expertise**

| *Area of Expertise* | *Credentials* | | | | *Method of Promotion* |
|---|---|---|---|---|---|
| | *Experience* | *Education* | *Awards* | *Other* | |
| | | | | | |
| | | | | | |
| | | | | | |
| | | | | | |
| | | | | | |
| | | | | | |

When one has made the effort to become an expert, it is only fair that one receives recognition for his or her expertise. If you have a professional qualification in a relevant discipline, if you've held a high-ranking position, if you've worked for a very successful company, or if you've been given a prestigious award, then people should know this.

Be particularly mindful of how you present this. There's a delicate balance between bragging and informing, and what is appropriate in one culture may not be appropriate in another. So, whatever you do to promote your image of expertise must be done in moderation. For instance, hanging an award certificate in your office, or writing articles for the trade press, may be good ways to show your expertise. Reminding people at every chance you get that you went to medical school—not so good.

I remember one consultant with whom I worked on a project with a client. When he ran out of things to say to defend a point for a strategy he was recommending, he adamantly stated, "I have an MBA!" as if that conferred some type of authority or something. I thought it was such an odd thing to say to a client as a defense of a strategy he was attempting to persuade the client to follow. Then I realized, he was in his fifties, but he had only graduated from the MBA program a few years before. When the client pushed back and said, "So do many others I could ask for assistance, but what makes you such an expert that I should trust your recommendation?" I was glad he didn't work for me. That would have been his final hour of employment. Firing people while on a project is such an awful responsibility of leadership, but that error was as egregious as a doctor about to risk injury to a patient by recommending a surgery that he wasn't qualified to recommend or perform. The other firm kept him on because they sent him out there alone without a mentor or a senior to monitor his interactions with a client.

Now, replace "I have an MBA" with "I have a medical license." If you are not promoting your expertise actively and using your charisma and referent power, why should others trust you as an expert? If you say nothing to promote your informal power in a market niche, then the sign on the wall says, "I have my medical license" and not much more. Now I will be brutal: That's what your competitors are saying to the market if all they do is establish a concierge practice that gives patients their phone number and email address and no waiting time, and same-day appointments, and blah, blah, blah amenities that everyone else in concierge medicine markets these days.

## Building Additional Expertise

Expert power starts with understanding your current skills and expertise. When you know your current areas of expertise, it's much easier for you to identify leadership roles where you'll be most successful. This same understanding also helps you hire consultants and leverage this insight to control the scope of work and deliverable from the consultant. Remember what I wrote earlier in the book: Consultants teach, coach, and mentor. Contractors *do* things. Some firms do both. The rate for contracting should never be the same as the rate for consulting. So if we can winnow down that which you need to know to expand your current expertise, we can work on continuing to grow and develop your expert power.

Think about the following:

1. **Expertise you need now:** The skills and knowledge you have now are excellent and a great start, but are they the skills that you need to be exceptionally effective (and respected) in your current role? Do you need to build additional areas of expertise? Which ones? If there's no time to learn them and you need something done right now, hire a contractor to do it for you.
2. **Expertise you'll need for the future:** When you look ahead to the next role you want to develop, do you have the skills that you'll need for this? Do you need another expert to vet your strategy and plan? A consultant is that sounding board, not a contractor. The contractor takes the instructions and specifications and does the job. The

> contractor doesn't decide what the job is supposed to be. When you don't know or are unsure about what you don't know, the consultant is the one to call.

However good your skills are right now, you should always be searching for skills that you'll need to develop to move your career in the direction you want.

**Expertise you want:** Equally, you may want to develop skills and expertise as part of your personal and professional development. You may be able to get by without a consultant or contractor for this. It may be as simple as buying and reading a few books (self-study), taking an online course, attending a seminar or workshop, or hiring a tutor or trainer. Consultants usually fill this role, but if it is a specific skill, a contractor may have just enough know-how to train you how to do a skill that is very specific.

As a physician, you maintain expertise by attending continuing medical education (CME) courses. When you have certain expertise, you have to work hard to maintain it and keep current.

The first step toward maintaining your expert power and your position in your market niche is to preserve your credibility. We all do this by understanding our limitations. Many people think that leaders need to know everything, but that thinking is flawed: exceptional leaders know whom to call and when to ask for help so they can accomplish what they set out to do.

Powerful experts are trusted to know *how* to achieve objectives they set for themselves and for others that follow them, but they don't need to know *how to do every task* that contributes to achieving those objectives. As a concierge physician, you may have a pregnant patient who requires the expertise of a surgeon who specializes in *in utero* surgery. Your patient trusts your insight and values your opinion about whom to call, when, and what she will be asked to do. She doesn't expect you to do the *in utero* surgery.

If you try to appear expert at something you're not, others will quickly see through this, and followers may start to question your niche expertise and ability to lead in areas where you really are knowledgeable.

Physicians are smart people. Smart people often have a tough time remembering that, although they know a lot about a subject or task, this doesn't translate to being better or smarter. Always take care to ensure that followers (patients, staff, and referring colleagues) feel comfortable expressing ideas and asking questions. Make an effort to appear approachable and open. This is especially true in concierge medicine because one of the amenities people pay for is the enhanced access to you. If you stay in your ivory tower, followers' claims that you sold something that you aren't delivering will have merit. The membership is paid so you will have more time for them (and their reams of Google search results).

## Building Influence as a Medical Expert in Your Market Niche Domain Area

Expert power is a positive kind of power; therefore you must make sure that you support your followers, protect their self-esteem, and avoid making them feel inferior or bashful. Expert power is related to another kind of power: the power to influence others. These others include your staff, the hospital executives up the road, the members of your concierge practice, and the public that is included as part of your target market that you hope to influence with your expertise such that they become disciples, followers of your influence as a member of your tribe, your concierge practice, and the teachings and counsel you provide as a thought leader and influencer of good health, prevention or mitigation of chronic disease, wellness, and patient engagement toward getting better when they are ill.

Once you learn how to build and use that influence skillfully, you will distinguish your brand from all other competitors in the market where you practice. This I can promise. After you learn how to use the influence, you get to choose your strategy and method of execution to apply that influence to build a thriving concierge private practice. Think of all the traditional practice physicians out there who don't get this opportunity. They chose not to do this for whatever reason. They are no longer your competition. You left them behind. You aren't looking for what they have anymore. You took the other fork in the road. This influence thing—they don't understand it, haven't thought about it, have no time for it, and aren't seeking it.

Building influence with patients and staff and colleagues starts with a need—the need to get something done. If there isn't anything to do or to change, there is no need for influence. It's an interesting word, *influence*. It means to cause an effect, to inspire, to change, to shape, to bring impact, to stimulate. So to get whatever it is that needs to be done, we sometimes may not have the power to exercise authority or impose our will in a situation. So to get something done, we exercise our ability to influence others.

Influence can also be described as *manipulation*. In medicine, often it is considered unethical to manipulate patients, so we rely on influence to get things done. Whether it's getting approval for a procedure to be carried out, to take a medication that may have rewards that outweigh the risks, or to get patients to commit to expenditures beyond their budget or insurance coverage. Your ability to influence others matters.

If you've ever witnessed someone without any real or legitimate authority achieve more than a person with a fancy title, you've witnessed the power of influence. Conversely, have you ever been in a position of authority, but still not felt powerful? You might have had the title *team leader* or *practice owner* or *partner* in a group practice, but if your staff or manager don't see you as an influential leader, you won't get much effort out of them. I've been a practice administrator for too many years and I can identify a lack of influence immediately in a practice. The first signs and symptoms of ineffective leadership and lack of influence are where the staff plays the two partners against one another or play the manager versus the partner or owner against one another in a game of "Go ask Mom" or "Go ask Dad." Patients who are drug seekers and attention seekers do it too, playing one doctor against another.

When this happens, it's important to step back and figure out what changes you can make to increase your personal influence. You need to figure out what you can do to become more influential and better able to convince others to support and follow you, especially if your name is on the signature line of the paychecks.

Influence comes from a variety of sources. How much expertise you have, how credible your position and objectives are, how visible you are, and how you align your objectives with your brand (the impression that others have about you and your practice, not your logo) all serve to increase your ability to have a positive influence on others.

As you attempt to build influence, there are three key things to consider:

- what contributes to personal influence and how to develop it
- how you can use specific sources of personal power to increase your influence, and
- specific strategies for making yourself more influential and better able to shape and control your work and your satisfaction with this new concierge style of healthcare delivery.

Influence, according to the *Merriam-Webster Dictionary*, is the "act or power of producing an effect without apparent force or direct authority." This dynamic between power and influence is an important element of successful business management and doctoring.

Influencc comes from personal power: some from the person that you are and some from the work that you do. This interesting and delicate balance is the point at which power and influence are intricately related and bound together. You can probably think of instances where a seemingly powerful person was not necessarily influential. I pointed to examples above for practice managers, partner physicians in a group practice, and you can probably think of medical staff leaders and hospital executives who come to mind. We all can. However, for a person to be influential, he or she has to have *some* power—formal or otherwise.

Expert power and influence with patients is a positive and productive thing. It is magical when used properly. It gets things done. It enhances patient engagement. It encourages people to care about themselves, their families, and their decisions. This is that difference between concierge medicine and traditional medicine—because influencing patients takes time and effort. Time that the 7-minute guys and gals don't have to give.

When used right, a high degree of influence can be viewed as a sign of personal and professional efficacy. Influential physicians often help shape positive health habits and motivate others to care for themselves. It also enables practice owners and partner physicians to motivate staff to deliver customer delight, not just customer service. This means that physicians and others with influence are viewed positively and others want to be around them. This influence makes it easier to sell memberships and renewals too!

If you are unable to influence, you will have difficulty in selling concierge memberships, because in essence, people are buying something (a membership) that satisfies their desire to have access to *the influencer*. They become angry at the traditional practice physician who keeps ignoring them or turning them down for appointments or prescription refills or time to ask questions, or they become apathetic and quit trying. Both are self-destructive and cause others to turn away.

So they turn toward your product. The *product* is the amenities-based membership. The CPT codes are the service, remember?

To build influence as a concierge physician with a market niche, you must develop and execute strategies to build influence as well as convert certain sources of power into interpersonal influence. Those who choose concierge medicine without this have little chance of distinguishing their brand from other *membership sellers*. You don't compete with these doctors either, but the market won't know that until you can execute a strategy that makes them aware (through integrated marketing, promotion, public

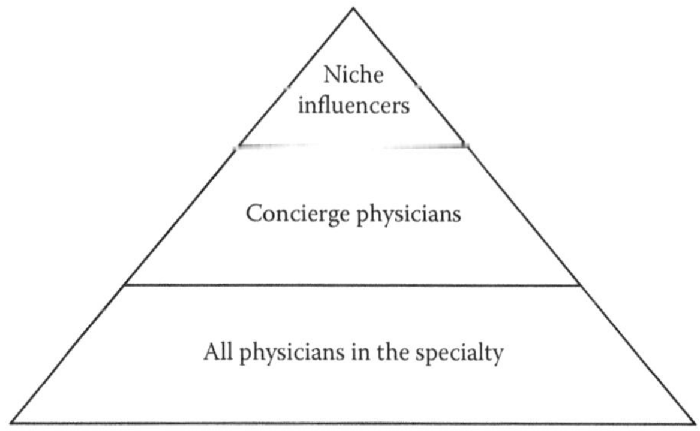


**Figure 5.1 Your pyramid of domain influence.**

relations, branding, and advertising) of that difference. The way I see this market competitive advantage is depicted in Figure 5.1.

At the base are all the physicians in the market—traditional and concierge. Then come those who launch a concierge or direct practice. They sell memberships or do something different from the ones at the base of the triangle. Then there are the ones who seek to differentiate their brand with niche market influence in a domain that aligns with their passion for a certain approach to medicine, a chronic illness grouping, or something else that they choose to claim. That is the domain of influence where you will compete, but first, you will have to educate the market on why and how you are different so that you can influence their filters.

Earlier in the chapter, we examined expert, referent, and other powers. Another form of power is *information power*, which comes from being informed. Being comes from actively learning. It is a result that comes from education—the education that comes from your marketing and marketing communications efforts. The expert power I covered earlier in the chapter is task-relevant knowledge or experience.

Part of the strategy for marketing and advertising that you will develop is the method you will use to carve yourself out of the second level of the triangle. This method will be the process whereby you build and use the respect that influences others. Building expert power takes time and effort; however, the payoff to your concierge practice will be significant. Remember, we are only looking for 300–600 unique people to influence in the community, not the whole community. If the market doesn't have 300–600 of them, chances are you will need another market to sell your product or you will have to raise your price in order to become sustainable and profitable.

There is a caution here about becoming too much of an expert. This can cause isolation. This is particularly the case if the expertise you've built is not relevant to the key niche market you've chosen to claim as your own, or if it's not valuable in the role to which you aspire as influencer of health treatments, prevention, and wellness or business owner.

I also covered *charismatic power* earlier in the chapter. This is the one source of power that you have that is different from all the rest because it refers to having socially desirable personal characteristics to which followers are drawn. Some people call it *personal magnetism*. Charismatic people are confident, assertive, and they have presence. They get noticed not because they are arrogant or conceited, but because of the strength of character they emit. The more people pay positive attention to you and like you, the more they will listen to you and the more personal power and influence you will have.

It is quite amusing to me when a new prospective client to build a concierge practice calls me to help him build or convert a practice. I check his social media rankings across the Internet. The comments are negative, he has one or two stars, and the comments are not about customer service or appointment availability, or some such other complaint. No. they are complaints about arrogance and conceit or indifference of the physician. Really? And they now want to charge people extra money for this? Good luck with that. Have you met my competitor? Here, let me introduce you. They are the St. Jude consulting firm—the patron saint of hopeless causes. If the arrogant and conceited doctor won't improve but just wants to start charging a membership fee to patients to be in their miserable practice—I know my limits. I am not a miracle worker.

Building your confidence, being passionate about your chosen niche, and living a life that is purposeful and exemplary all coincide with exuding charisma. Other things you can do to build charisma include adopting agreeable behaviors with referring patients and colleagues, nurses at the hospital, and maintaining impeccable clothes and grooming. (That's packaging, which is part of the advertising.) Don't believe me? Consider this difference: Scrubs that look like blue pajamas or tailored apparel—which is more the mark of success that breeds influence? But while these might enhance your charisma, there is also a limit to how far you can go with them if you are not naturally charismatic. At a fundamental level, charisma is something very cut and dried. You either have it or you don't. That's why using it as a strategy to gain influence is different from using a strategy to gain charisma. The other issue is that if this is your primary source of influence, it may not last long. You will need to have substantive expertise that is better developed by other means.

When we consider engagements with physicians who want to build a concierge practice, there are certain elements we look for, including the following:

- A good work ethic
- A higher than expected commitment to building a thriving concierge practice
- The willingness to work on the assigned tasks that it takes to design, launch, and build the practice
- Attention to the details that the practice managers already hired or who will be hired won't have time or skill to carry out
- Value Congruence—this is behavior that is consistent with the brand they believe they own. Do they walk the talk?
- Centrality—are they the hub of information and communication? Are they the doctor that the market believes is *in the know*? Do they have a network of followers and referral sources that trust them for being *in the know* about something?
- Flexibility—how much discretion do they have to build a concierge practice? If their employment contract where they currently work (a group practice, the hospital, the urgent care center, the public health clinic, etc.) restricts this flexibility to choose to do something different with the relationships they currently have established with patients, they may not have the flexibility to choose to apply their influence. Those who do what they are told or have agreed to do something in accordance with a noncompete or noncircumvention contract, are not perceived as having much power and influence.
- Are they creative and innovative?
- Visibility—do other market leaders and other powerful and influential people see their influence? The more people to whom they can demonstrate their competence, the better. Sometimes this can be improved with a good public relations strategy. If they are able to foster solid relationships with community business and local and regional health leaders, all the better. If a concierge physician doesn't have the time to do this on his own or know how to do it, then a hired contractor can be assigned to arrange invitations for him to participate in meetings and other events where influential people are gathered. The public relations

contractor will work on assigned tasks that increase the concierge physician's face-to-face communication and direct contact with senior influencers in the community. A consultant may be called upon to develop the strategy and action plan that the contractor will carry out. And again, I want to emphasize, don't allow yourself to be taken advantage of by paying higher hourly rates for consultants who charge higher rates for developing a strategy when a contractor carries out the steps to execute the strategy on your behalf. The rate for the public relations person to call on the phone and make inroads and opportunities is a lower contract rate, often paid on a performance basis, not hourly. The important point here is that the visibility has to happen. If the doctor won't do it himself, or appoints a person who is incapable, the strategy won't execute itself. If I see telltale signs of this on the initial interview and consultation, I have grave reservations about the viability of the conversion and the potential for the practice to thrive.

- Relevance—this is how well your expertise and efforts to promote your expert power are aligned with your brand touch points. The more your work is associated with issues central to the success of your brand, the greater your personal influence.

## Using Your Power and Influence

Having a high degree of expert power, charisma, and influence will still not be enough to make your concierge practice thrive. You also have to develop the skill to use it effectively. You can be a popular concierge doctor with a banner first year as a result of an effective sales strategy, but you will lose many members on renewal if you don't know how to relate to your patients and get them to use their concierge membership to its fullest potential. All your expert power will be ineffectual. As a concierge physician in this business model, what is important to your business success will be your ability and that of your nurse practitioner, physician assistant, or your nurses and office staff to get your members to work *with* you to accomplish their wellness and treatment goals.

A great strategy for gaining influence with coworkers and subordinates is to use reason. This means gaining commitment through a shared understanding. Commitment relies on explaining legitimate needs and then trusting the good intent of others to work with you. Using reason rests on your ability to persuade others using facts, needs, and personal values as the basis for your argument. Think about it. When you write a prescription or patient instructions, you are in essence saying to your patients,

- "I want you to ____ because it's good for/necessary to/consistent with …"
- "The literature supports my recommendation that you …"
- "By agreeing to do this, you will meet your own personal objectives …"

You phrase your recommendation or prescription in a way that is consistent with their needs and their values, don't you? This is ethical and good medicine. It is transparent, and affords them the opportunity to allow themselves to *be influenced* by you. The key to using persuasion effectively is allowing the other person to use her own good judgment and respecting their need to feel empowered in her decision to go along with your recommendations as her doctor.

In conjunction with the rational argument for what you recommend as their personal physician, you can also use an inspirational appeal to influence them. They have already paid their membership money to be a member of your "club" and listen to what you recommend. They want to pay attention to what you have to say because you're seen as influential. This transcends not just office visits, but your newsletter messages, your blog, and all your communications and interactions. When you combine that communication with inspiration, you motivate your concierge members, your colleagues that send you referrals, and those who read your blog and newsletter and may make a decision to become concierge members later on. You will find it easy to build passion, excitement, enthusiasm, and commitment to better health and wellness, which becomes the essence of your brand.

Before you move forward in this chapter, take a moment to ponder the following. There are no right or wrong answers. The answers are deeply personal. How you choose to take action on them is totally dependent on you and what you want to achieve for your concierge practice.

- If you've decided on a niche market, where do you feel you lack influence and power right now?
- What can you do to increase your sense of control and empowerment?
- Write down some ways that you become more influential.
- Close your eyes and focus on envisioning yourself with more personal and professional influence; describe how you feel and what you did to make it happen.
- Jot down some ideas that you can turn into a plan to bring your vision to life.

When you use your expert power in concierge medicine, you will see just how natural it feels to *influence, persuade*, and *motivate* others. Be cognizant that you are doing this; don't become desensitized to this power. As a concierge physician, you have promised that in exchange for the membership fee, you will take the time and seize the opportunity to make use of rational persuasion—the use of logical arguments and facts—to convince patients to engage in their health and wellness decisions and to join you (referent power) or agree with you (leadership). However, this assumes that your information will be objective, evidence based, and accurate. Therefore, it is essential that you remain current with what's happening in your market niche domain of expertise. Otherwise, your expertise will be questioned, and your ability to influence others will be compromised. That's the first step to a disenrollment and a vote of *no confidence.*

One of the reasons why I urge concierge physicians to become active in blogging and newsletters or coffee-break emails is because of how important it is to remain connected to members. You must always remain approachable and connected to your concierge members, fans, followers, and even the patients who didn't follow you through your transition to concierge medicine. They may still follow eventually. If you distance yourself from your followers, you'll likely stop sharing and communicating your expertise. This makes it very difficult for you to influence your team, your patients, and your referral sources, as you won't be aware of what motivates or inspires them.

What's more, be humble in your approach with everyone: practice patience, and take time to coach people when they need it. And, as far as you sensibly can, let people work out solutions for themselves, and let them keep ownership of their ideas. That's part of the healing too.

Medicine is laden with crises. Wellness and health maintenance is just dandy, but the rubber meets the road in a crisis. That's when your followers will look to you for your expertise and guidance. Being confident in a crisis is perhaps the toughest technique to practice out of the three that I am highlighting here. When a crisis occurs, your staff, patients, and even your colleagues will look to you for direction, motivation, and inspiration. As an expert, you're expected to know what to do, and you must meet that expectation in order to maintain your expert status.

Medicine is not an exact science. In many crises, you don't need to find a perfect solution: a good solution is often enough. In fact, the precise final outcome of your decision can be less important than your willingness to take the lead on care and treatment recommendations. You are recommending, you are not mandating. People still get to make choices. They take responsibility for their choices and they suffer the consequences of their choices if they make bad ones. They look to your expertise to explain their options, and transfer power to you based on their belief in your expertise.

So today, think about how you will take your chosen market niche, develop your expertise, and use this expert power to achieve buy-in from staffers, referral sources, hospital administrators, concierge members, and those who may become concierge members in your practice or recommend others in the future. When you use expert power as your power base, or as a complement to other formal and informal sources of power, you will find that it is easier to build on the trust and respect that your expertise provides, and make a positive impact on your staff, your patients, and your followers as a concierge physician with a thriving private medicine practice. I promise you that this will differentiate your concierge practice from the rest of your competitors.

# Chapter 6

# Clarifying Your Business Concept: Welcome to the Next Chapter of Your Professional Life

Starting a business is exciting! So often, we receive calls from physicians who are frustrated with what has become of healthcare, their career, their practice revenues and overheads, and their work–life balance. If you have already decided to launch a concierge or direct practice, all that is about to change for you.

In the previous chapters, we worked on the ideal practice vision, what you want it to be, and we worked on some introspective insights and your reason for taking this step, and what you hope to achieve through expert power, influence, and charisma.

## Working with Consultants and Contractors to Get You Started

This next section is not meant to be self-serving, by any means. I included it because it is highly likely that you will ask several consultants (lawyers, accountants, and other specialized consultants) for help and guidance. You have to know how to best work with a consultant, or you might be taken advantage of by those who sell good words, but have only greed as a goal, preying on the rich doctors who have more money than sense.

You may not be all that familiar with how consultants and contractors can play a role to help you clarify and execute your business concept. If the people you plan to hire to help you clarify your business concept are incapable of writing or discussing what I covered in Chapter 5, at the level of knowledge of how concierge medicine works and what it takes to differentiate your concierge brand, think hard about whether you want them guiding anything else about your business.

There are a small number of good consultants who specialize in developing this kind of a practice. They are available to assist you and be supportive like a business startup Sherpa. Your consultants' roles are to act as a guide to facilitate your journey across the mountain peaks you are about to negotiate in the development of your business.

If you outsource certain tasks, that is the role of a contractor, not a consultant. The two are very different. If you jumped to this section of the book without reading the previous chapters, you missed my view on the difference between consultants and contractors. One advises about things, and helps you make decisions by calling on professional training and experience. The other *does* things by the hour. Consultants sometimes direct the work of contractors or help you design the scope of work that the contractor will do for you. Knowing the difference between the two can save you time and money and avoid costly mistakes and poor guidance.

In our firm, we employ both consultants and contractors. In addition to guiding you and providing instruction and insight, if you get tired, overwhelmed, can't manage something, or simply don't want to do a task, you can hand it over to us for assistance. Not all firms do this, and some who do it charge the same for contract assistance as they do for consulting. This is not in your best interest. Consultants charge for their knowledge and expertise. Contractors should be paid mid-market to top-market rate for the job they are doing, plus about 40–45% to cover margins, overheads, and expenses usually paid by an employer.

Contractors work on a deliverable or a list of deliverables, produced in a certain time frame. They work by a specification called a scope of work (SOW). They are often not paid on retainer, but instead hired by the hour or the project. They may ask for a deposit and tranche funding (paid in time increments or at project milestones). In most cases, you will be charged for any expenses incurred or paid out on your behalf.

## The Difference between a Concierge Medicine Product and Medical Services

Let's look at this in a parallel to what you are about to create. As a concierge physician, you will have certain amenity-based services, such as answering questions after hours, easy access to you and the information you can provide, and other services not described by a CPT code. That is the concierge side of the business. That is what is paid for by the membership fee.

The contractor side of the business can be described by CPT codes. They are the medical services you offer, making diagnoses based on patient examinations, complaints, labs, x-rays, etc., as well as any procedures you may perform or may be performed by your staff under your supervision. There is a market rate for the contract services, usually a percentage of a percentile of the usual and customary fee schedules of your managed care plans, Medicare, and other reference standards. The concierge membership fee is based on what the market will bear, and if the market sees your offer as valuable enough to pay money for it. This is very much similar to how we charge for our consulting services.

Like you, a consultant adds a certain value or benefit to a project when the consultant engages with a client on a project.

There are two primary types of consultants out there—generalists and specialists. The past few chapters and exercises, especially in Chapter 5, have focused on identifying and developing your specialized market niche. Similarly, there are consultants out there that are strategy generalists (McKinsey, Bain, and BCG, Deloitte, etc.), and then there are technical or specialty shops like ours, mostly boutique firms.

The generalist firms bring brand name opinions to a project. These are used for certain things:

1. **Political leverage:** When a hospital CEO needs to "blame the other guy" or the "experts" for an unpopular decision, his organization often brings in a consulting firm to take the blame. This provides ammunition to recommend an unpopular or risky decision to the board (expansion into a new business line or geography, or shutting down a department or service line). This blame is staged, known in advance, and well compensated. Finally, if things go wrong, consultants are a handy scapegoat and are insured for millions of dollars in the event a scandal ensues, a public relations nightmare erupts, the media makes a mockery of the

scapegoat (remember Andersen and Enron?), or some other malpractice liability is assigned. As a result, their rates reflect these insurance premiums and the costs to maintain the brand

2. **Pooled knowledge across functions:** When consultants from generalist firms engage on a project, they have to *learn* the client's culture, politics, and organization culture. Usually, the entire first month is spent building a fact base. This is done by interviewing people across functions, much the same as a physician does when conducting a comprehensive history and physical. See the example in Table 6.1 to understand my thinking on this analogy.

   In large companies, cross-functional problem solving rarely happens. Just getting different functions in a room typically unlocks creative problem solving. You can also see that this not necessary for a contractor, but it will be necessary for a consultant to know. The consultant uses this information to figure out or confirm what needs to be done by the client or its contractors. The consultant can bring more value to the project the more the consultant knows about the client. If your consultant doesn't take this step before he or she starts recommending actions and strategies, *run*. You have encountered a consultant imposter! There are many of them out there. People can say they are a consultant just so that they don't have to explain why they are out of a job.

   Just as no physician would treat a patient without a relevant H&P (history and physical) and the competency to evaluate what they learn, no consultant should prescribe actions and investments and strategies that will affect your business without knowing this much about you. A contractor, on the other hand, simply waits for your instructions on what you want him to *do*. He doesn't do diagnosis or strategy.

3. **Pool knowledge across levels:** Similarly, consultants from generalist consulting firms interview, watch, and tag along with people down the organization's structure, often starting with customers and moving through formal department or job roles. CEOs and the executive teams of the larger generalist firms rarely do this (exception for their largest customers). There are tremendous insights to be had by doing this.

4. **Deep focus on one problem:** The biggest value that a large generalist firm can bring is that it can assign a dedicated team of pretty smart people who are generally unbiased who can focus deeply on one particular problem. The problem you'll encounter here is that those smart people come at a high price per hour. Often, one is a team leader and the rest are fresh graduates who may have no experience, but bill out at

**Table 6.1 Comprehensive Client Fact Base**

| **Identifying data:** Age, gender, marital status | **Client information:** |
|---|---|
| **Chief complaint:** | **Scope of the project:** |
| What brought you to the hospital? | Why did you call a consultant? |
| **HPI:** | **History of the business:** |
| When did it start? | When did it start? |
| Where did it start (physically)? | Where did it start (physically)? |
| What does it feel like (characterize pain)? | Brand characteristics |
| Can you rate pain on a scale of 1–10? | Market share |
| How often? How long? How many? | What has changed? |
| In what setting did this occur (surrounding environment/context)? | Surrounding factors |
| Does anything make it worse/better? | What works, what doesn't? |
| Did you notice anything associated with the primary symptom? | Was there anything else? |
| **Medications:** | **What has been done to date?** |
| What meds? | Action |
| What dose? | Steps taken |
| What route? | Strategy |
| What frequency? | For how long was it attempted? |
| Results? | Outcomes |
| **Allergies:** | **Company politics:** |
| Are you allergic to any medications/ever had a reaction to any medication? | Known corporate taboos and positions or sensitivities |
| Any food/environmental allergies? | Any specific topics or areas to avoid? |
| **Tobacco/Alcohol/Drugs:** | **Special programs ongoing:** |
| Can be asked here or in personal/social history (Hx) | Social responsibility |
| Do you smoke? How long? How much? How often? | Political activism |

*continued*

**Table 6.1 (continued) Comprehensive Client Fact Base**

| | |
|---|---|
| Can you tell me about your drinking habits? | Public relations issues |
| Do you use illicit drugs? | |
| **Past History:** | **Past History:** |
| ***Childhood*** | ***During startup*** |
| Did you have any major childhood illnesses (mumps/measles/chicken pox)? | What "bumps in the road" were encountered? |
| Any chronic childhood illnesses? | Policies or cultures established? |
| ***Adult*** | ***After 5 years*** |
| Medical: Have you been diagnosed with any illnesses as an adult (diabetes, hypertension, hepatitis, etc.)? | Known problems in the business |
| Surgical: Can you tell me about any major surgeries you've had? When? For what? What type of operation? | Interventions undertaken and results |
| Ob/Gyn: Any pregnancies? | New service lines or endeavors |
| Can you tell me about your menstruation history? Onset, describe cycle? How's your sexual function? | Operational day-to-day issues |
| Psychiatric: Any history of psychiatric illness? (Diagnosis, hospitalization, treatment) | Corporate cultures or informal cultures present |
| Have you gotten your immunizations (tetanus, polio, etc.)? | How often does the firm evaluate strategy and make preventive tweaks? |
| TB, pap smear, mammogram, cholesterol? | Routine KPIs measured |
| **Family Hx:** | **Corporate Family** |
| Can you tell me a bit about your father's health (age, or cause of death)? Diagnosed with anything? | CEO profile |

**Table 6.1 (continued) Comprehensive Client Fact Base**

| | | |
|---|---|---|
| How about your mother? | COO profile | |
| Brothers? | Other C-suite profiles | |
| Sisters? | Finance | Technology |
| Grandparents? | Strategy | Chief Medical |
| Grandchildren? | Compliance | Chief Nursing |
| Any history of hypertension, stroke, diabetes, thyroid/renal disease? Arthritis, TB, lung disease, mental illness (suicide), substance abuse? | Any history of problems, issues, or recognition in the community as a leader? | |
| **Personal/Social History:** | **The Individual Physician** | |
| What do you do for a living? | Specialty and niche favorites | |
| How far along in school did you get? | Areas of special competency | |
| What is it like at home? | Home life | |
| Any significant others? How is the relationship? | S/O/Marital situation | |
| Any significant sources of stress (immediate/ongoing)? | Stressors | |
| Religious/spiritual beliefs? | Spiritual influences (no abortion, etc.) | |
| Activities of daily living (especially elderly)? | ADLs (sports, lifestyle, Internet savvy) | |
| Do you exercise much? | Exercise level | |
| What is your usual daily food intake? Caffeine? | Eating habits | |
| Any alternative healthcare? | Complementary and alternative medicine acceptance, interest, or competency | |
| **Review of Systems** | **Review of Departments in the Firm** | |

an exorbitant fee per hour. Will you be paying for their on-the-job training? What value do they bring?

The old joke is that consultants tell you what you already know and then charge you for it. Fair enough, but the real value that impacts the bottom line, no matter how you measure it, is that an absence of strong leadership or a big, risky culture change, often cannot be accomplished without the consultant for guidance, avoiding mistakes, shortening learning curves, or supplying information you would otherwise have to develop through time and formal learning. In essence, consultants bring valuable general and specific experience and boutique firms often bring subject matter expertise that is not otherwise available at generalist consulting firms. This is similar to the market niche approach we discussed in Chapter 5, and why your concierge medical niche practice, in all likelihood, offers better value than a generalist concierge medical practice.

5. **Subject matter expertise:** The people who are doing the bulk of the work at the big generalist firms and many of the mid-size boutique firms are fresh out of college or business school, often from a range of majors, with little-to-no work experience. They are usually really smart, very hard working, resourceful, and well trained, but they don't know anything about your medical practice, the art of running a practice, marketing a practice, or compliance issues that arise in the operation of a medical practice. More interestingly, the director or partner on the project is not really a subject matter expert either. Often that project or team leader has built a career in a particular industry or practice area and has served a range of clients across a range of problems.

   The value that the large consulting firm's director or partner brings to the project is *pattern recognition*, but there is no way that he or she can know more about your situation, practice, or particular set of challenges, compared to a real subject matter expert who is involved in that problem every single day for years. This is analogous to what we are trying to build for you and your market niche concierge practice. We want to position you as the subject matter expert in your chosen domain. Last, most partners and directors at generalist firms are career consultants, not industry veterans. (This is particularly true at the big generalist firms.) Be careful when selecting a consultant as your coach and mentor.

6. **Retainers:** The big consulting firms love to provide long-term, ongoing, ambiguous projects on a retainer, and their contracts are often written so that there is no deliverable other than to "be available." This sounds like some concierge physician membership contracts I've encountered. Patients don't want to pay $1200–$1800 a year for you to spend a half hour a month on an occasional call anymore than you want the partner or senior consultant of a firm thinking about you or your problem in order to bill you on a retainer. If you hire on the basis of a retainer, state what the deliverable is that makes sense to you.
7. **Actual decision making:** Consultants are great at assembling facts from outside your practice and inside from your data. They bring perspective from all functions and levels of your company, finding interesting patterns, and providing you with a point of view. However, they cannot or should not make the tough decisions for you. No outsider can ever truly understand your thinking as the primary stakeholder of your new concierge medical practice because no outsider has as much at stake personally and professionally. Only you can pull the trigger for your concierge medical practice; the consultant can, at best, show you how to hold the gun and maybe give you a few targets to aim at. Again, this is similar to how you will act as a coach and mentor to your concierge patients. You may give great coaching and guidance, but it will take effort on the part of the body-owner to choose the apple over the doughnut.

Here are some things you may wish to prepare before you engage a consultant.

1. **Impose limits:** Make sure that you specifically define a narrow problem with which you want the consultant to help, well before the consultant is engaged. Make sure it's a project of defined length, with a defined number and type of resource. Demand frequent updates and check-ins. Have the option of aborting the project if you are not getting what you want or if the directional answer is not specific enough.

   For example, when I consult with a new concierge physician client, I come for an initial visit and assessment. That is the beginning and the ending of the engagement for that task. I ask questions and make recommendations based on experience and high-level unique research. I travel to the client's location, which incurs an expense to me whether I drive or fly and stay overnight in order to get an early start, or have to stay two nights because of airline itineraries in some of the more challenging locations. As a deliverable, I leave behind worksheets, tools, and a punch-list that was developed over years of experience. Clients tell us that the benefit of our fast-track checklist is that it enables clients to start imposing these defined scope limits and helps them articulate what they want consultants to solve or contractors to produce. The problem it solves is filling in the gaps of the information that the client doesn't know that they don't know. Many of these tools were used to produce the content of this book, but without the skills and time to use them, they are just words on a page.

2. **Use a bid process:** To sort out the subject matter experts from the generalists, create a request for proposal (RFP). Put them through a competitive bid process (sealed bid or auction) with preset milestones.

   Avoid attempting to get free information and recommendations through the RFP process. For example, I had a prospect call me and ask me what value I bring to the table and had me write the bullet points of what I could supply. From this, I am sure he planned to create his RFP or use it for his business plan as his strategy of what needed to be done. I wrote it up, and supplied it in the most general sense. Then he came back with a second round of questions, asking for more detail on each bullet point. I responded with even higher level information. A few months later, I was able to obtain a copy of his business plan from someone. Lo and behold, all my bullet points and my explanations were there as his intellectual property. Since I marked my proposal for internal use only, not to be re-released without the express written consent of the author, as soon as he got funding, we sued—and won on a copyright violation. To do that is bad faith, nefarious, and theft of intellectual property. He did not pay us for the information or the permission to use it. He paid a lot more because I could connect the use to a benefit such as funding the project for which he used our methods and copyrighted information in an unethical and illegal way.

   Prospects will tell you that they don't participate in auctions.

   Sometimes, consultants will try to circumvent your limitations and scope by attempting to define your problem differently or changing the milestones so that they can add more to the scope for a bigger bill. Don't do it. Force the standardized process so you can make an objective comparison. The parallel here is that you will be offering a scope of services under your concierge membership agreement. You will be compared to others offering a concierge membership product. Are you going to add and subtract items from your list of services that a concierge patient is entitled to, and juggle the price of membership against what others will offer on a one-off basis? That would be silly!

3. **Demand partner time:** When you hire a consulting firm, whose name is on the door? If it is my firm, my name is on the door as a principal. You get my attention, and you may also get attention from my assistances and colleagues. Would you rather spend time with someone with 30 years of consulting experience who has at least seen your problem in a different market or knows anything about your situation better than a 24-year-old with a fresh diploma who has never actually made a business decision? Consulting firms provide real business value; physicians just need to know how to appropriately use these service providers.

   The parallel here is similar to what you are selling. Are you selling a concierge membership that entitles the member to see your physician assistant or nurse practitioner? Or to see you? If the majority of the work will be done by an extender and not the physician (the model currently promoted by Signature MD, as I learned by attending their sales presentation), the value perceived by some patients may be very different than the value of having the partner or principal clinician at their disposal in exchange for the fee.)

4. **Conformist vs. disruptive orientation:** The longer a consultant partner or director remains at a big generalist firm, the more conformist he or she becomes. Conformists blend well into existing rules and never stand out, fit well in hierarchy, the crowd, and protect the bureaucratic hierarchical organizations. They will resonate with most hospital administrators, especially those who don't want the status quo to change. They do this because of a need to stay on the corporate track.

   On the other hand, disruptors are anti-conformists: they tend to avoid rules associated with traditional thinking, they try to grasp the essence of reality. Disruptors exude higher energy, are comfortable with paradigm shifts, innovation, critical thinking, and dispute or argument by choosing to investigate a topic; collect, generate, and evaluate evidence; and establish a position on the topic in a concise manner.

   Your concierge practice will be seen as disruptive among the traditional practice business models and you may find that you resonate better with the disruptor orientation.

## A Consultant Should Never Assume What You Want

We can't assume what you want for your business or what you hope for. We have to ask.

Throughout this book, all the answers you give are fine, and you won't be judged. Your consultant may not always agree with you, and may push back, play devil's advocate, and challenge you to articulate your thinking a little better, but none of those responses should ever be interpreted as judgmental. Consultants come ready to stretch you to just beyond your comfort zone to reach new heights. Just don't give your copy of this book away if you write answers in it. You don't want your buddy copying your homework. Be a buddy, buy him or her their own copy as a gift.

As you plan and launch your new concierge practice, it is important to clarify and evaluate the viability of your business concept. This includes articulating your long-term vision, your personal goals, what you see as your business opportunity, and how you define certain objectives and business specifics. Consultants should never influence these. The consultant's role is to bring them to life, the easiest and most efficient way possible for you. You only need the consultant for this to the extent the consultant will add value or save you time or help you avoid mistakes.

Some physician entrepreneurs fancy themselves as "visionaries" because they see grand schemes and big pictures. They envision their concierge practice beating out the competition, racing to the max capacity of the practice membership in the first 6 months, defining new terms of art, new healthcare delivery styles, new membership programs, etc. Your business does not have to be radical or even original. It just has to answer a market need and be reflective of you and your brand—and sell 300–600 memberships.

Besides, over the course of time, your vision is going to evolve and adapt to the market as it finds its "legs" under the new epoch of healthcare reform in North America, for however long this one lasts. What seems really important to you and to your business vision now, may change radically in the next 3 to 5 years.

So in this next section, we will work hard on clarifying your current thinking about your concierge medical practice business vision, concepts, goals, and build the foundation upon which a viable, adaptable, and flexible model will be created that reflects your personal *brand* of healthcare business.

## Exercise 1: Goal Setting

### First-year basic goals for starting my practice

| | |
|---|---|
| Number of employees | |
| Number of locations | |
| Annual revenues | |
| Profits or profit margin | |
| Number of memberships | |
| Number of services and products we offer | |
| Ownership allocation | |
| Other goals | |

### Three-year goals for operating my practice

| | |
|---|---|
| Number of employees | |
| Number of locations | |
| Annual revenues | |
| Profits or profit margin | |
| Number of memberships | |
| Number of services and products we offer | |
| Ownership allocation | |
| Other goals | |

### Five-year goals for operating my practice

| | |
|---|---|
| Number of employees | |
| Number of locations | |
| Annual revenues | |
| Profits or profit margin | |
| Number of memberships | |
| Number of services and products we offer | |
| Ownership allocation | |
| Other goals | |

**Ten-year goals for operating my practice**

| | |
|---|---|
| Number of employees | |
| Number of locations | |
| Annual revenues | |
| Profits or profit margin | |
| Number of memberships | |
| Number of services and products we offer | |
| Ownership allocation | |
| Other goals | |

## Exercise 2: Business Priorities

### My Priorities for the New Practice

| *Goal* | *Urgent* | *Important* | *Eventually* | *Not on the Radar* | *Unimportant* |
|---|---|---|---|---|---|
| Add employees | | | | | |
| Add new service lines | | | | | |
| Increase marketing | | | | | |
| Add locations | | | | | |
| Add capacity | | | | | |
| Increase salaries | | | | | |
| Increase profit | | | | | |
| Retire debts and loans | | | | | |
| Increased cash reserves | | | | | |
| Acquire other practices | | | | | |
| | | | | | |
| | | | | | |
| | | | | | |

## Exercise 3: Motivating Factors

What motivates you the most? Order these by rank.

| *Creativity* | *Rank* |
|---|---|
| Determining my brand image | |
| Creating new services and products | |
| Devising new business policies and procedures | |
| Identifying new business opportunities | |
| Creating new business and patient education materials | |
| Devising new ways of doing old things | |
| *Control* | |
| Over my own work responsibilities | |
| Over my own time and work hours | |
| Over company decisions and directions | |
| Over products and services | |
| Over brand integrity | |
| Over other doctors | |
| Over other employees | |
| Over my work environment | |
| Over social/environmental impact of products and services | |
| Over my own business future | |
| Over the income I generate and how I generate it | |
| *Challenge* | |
| Long-term problem solving | |
| Critical problem solving (putting out fires) | |
| Handling many issues at once | |
| Continually dealing with new issues | |
| Perfecting solutions, clinical pathways, treatment protocols | |
| Organizing diverse cases and complicated care management | |

| *Cash* | |
|---|---|
| Income needed currently | |
| Income desired in 12–24 months | |
| Income desired in 25–60 months | |
| Wealth desired in 2–5 years (value of stocks or the company) | |

## Exercise 4: Articulating My Business Values

Describe the values that are important to you in building your practice, as they relate to the items in this chart:

| Corporate culture and nature of the work environment | |
|---|---|
| Business ethics | |
| Customer service (your corporate ethos) | |
| Vendor relations (your views on credit and debt) | |
| Advertising messages (What message do you want others to hear?) | |
| Employee treatment (wages, benefits, layoffs, promotions, empowerment, etc.) | |
| Community and civic involvement (your visibility and contributions) | |
| Environmental sustainability (your corporate ethos) | |

## Exercise 5: My Role Models—Who Do I Admire?

| *Name and Job Role* | *What Traits Do You Admire?* | *How Could You Incorporate Those Traits in Your Business?* |
|---|---|---|
| | | |
| | | |
| | | |
| | | |
| | | |

## Exercise 6: Identifying That Which Excites You about Your Concierge Medicine Practice Idea

| **What is your first idea?** | **What is your second idea?** | **What is your third idea?** |
|---|---|---|
| | | |
| **How did you come up with it?** | **How did you come up with it?** | **How did you come up with it?** |
| | | |
| **What excites you about it?** | **What excites you about it?** | **What excites you about it?** |
| | | |

This is what you will use to take your ideas and turn them into a plan, which becomes a successful business. You will also find it useful to refer to when you develop the content for the "About Us" part of your website.

## Exercise 7: Your Business Concept

It's more than a concierge medical practice.

<table>
<tr><td>Does it sell memberships?</td><td></td></tr>
<tr><td>Does it offer a package of amenity-based services in addition to medical treatments? If yes, which ones?</td><td>How many packaged programs will you offer?<br>❑ Executive Health<br>❑ Pediatrics?<br>❑ Alternative Medicine?<br>❑ Women's Health<br>❑ Longevity and Anti-Aging?<br>❑ Regenerative Medicine (Stem Cells)<br>❑ Family Programs?<br>❑ Couples Programs?<br>❑ Nutrition?<br>❑ Diagnostic Testing?<br>❑ House Calls?<br>❑ Travel Attendance?<br>❑ New Technology?<br>❑ Mobile Health Visits?<br>❑ DNA/Genome Testing?<br>❑ Molecular Medicine Testing?</td></tr>
<tr><td colspan="2">What improved services and features will you provide that your competitors don't offer?</td></tr>
<tr><td colspan="2">What makes your brand unique or special?</td></tr>
</table>

<table>
<tr><td colspan="5">Describe your potential customers:<br>• Age:<br>• Gender:<br>• Occupation:<br>• Socioeconomic Status:</td><td colspan="5">Patient engagement level:<br>• Average Household Income:<br>• Children in the Home:<br>• Marital Status:<br>• Political Leanings:</td></tr>
<tr><td colspan="5">Education Level:</td><td colspan="5">Primary Diseases:</td></tr>
<tr><td colspan="10">What will be your overall marketing and sales strategy (high level—we'll help you get granular)? How will you plan to sell memberships and connect with the market to let them know you are ready to be of service?</td></tr>
<tr><td colspan="10">Name your top 10 competitors in the area—(If you need help, we can research this for you.)</td></tr>
<tr><td colspan="2">1</td><td colspan="2">3</td><td colspan="2">5</td><td colspan="2">7</td><td colspan="2">9</td></tr>
<tr><td colspan="2">2</td><td colspan="2">4</td><td colspan="2">6</td><td colspan="2">8</td><td colspan="2">10</td></tr>
<tr><td colspan="10">What do you think will make customers buy from you rather than your competitors?</td></tr>
<tr><td colspan="10"></td></tr>
<tr><td colspan="10"></td></tr>
<tr><td colspan="10"></td></tr>
<tr><td colspan="10"></td></tr>
</table>

| What will you solve for the market? What segment is underserved and how? |
|---|
| |
| How do you plan to use the Internet for marketing your business? |
| |
| How will you use social media to market your business? |
| |
| **Provide one-sentence answers in 160-character snippets:** |
| Your core business concept: |
| Your core business values: |
| Your core business goals: |
| Your core financial goals: |
| Your corporate culture: |
| Now create an 800-character paragraph: We'll use this on the web and in your business summary, brand standard, and employee handbook. |
| |

Your concept has to be strong in at least one area, or you won't be able to describe how you will be truly competitive. If you don't have exact answers now, *just write down what you can. We will do more with this in Sprint #2.*

## Exercise 8: Testing Market Preferences for Your Concierge Amenities Package & Price Point

I've used this exercise with many client physicians with plans to transition an established practice.

1. First, call upon 10–15 patients (5–6 couples) whose opinions you respect and trust, selected from your "most likely to sign up" list.
2. Compose a letter inviting them to participate on a marketing research panel for a date 3 to 6 weeks in advance, on an evening or a Saturday morning. Make it at a location where you can seat the patients (couples, preferably) at a conference roundtable.
3. Start the program with a confidentiality agreement signature, that what they hear stays in the room, and is not to be shared with others outside the room.
4. Next, explain the concept of your model of concierge or direct practice medicine. Be clear that this is market research and has not yet been decided, and that you respect their insight, opinions, objectivity, etc. Allow them to ask any questions but not cross talk about their opinions. (Trust me on this!)
5. Dismiss the group to enjoy some light, healthful refreshments and distribute some SWAG (stuff we all get) to take home, including a gift card for about $15 for a coffee shop or grocery store, etc., some sunscreen, hand-sanitizer, etc.
6. Study your results.
7. Repeat this exercise with 3 or 4 groups of different ages, demographics, and lifestyles.

### *How to Gather Data without a Melee*

Have items for them to share their opinions. These could include, among other things:

- Name options: have them to rank order the name options on a tally sheet
- Service level options: ask them to tic boxes of things that are relevant to them
- Price points: allow them to suggest the value rather than pick from a list
- Amenities that are important to them and why: a place to write their opinions about the value of certain (or all) the amenities you are considering.

### *What to Do after the Decision to Move Forward*

Offer a coupon in their SWAG bag as a thank you gesture for $100 off their membership (per person) should you decide to move forward with your plans to transition to concierge medicine. Classify the membership as Diamond or some such other level indicating their special recognition as a part of your launch strategy. Only participants at the Delphi sessions can be Diamond level so that there's exclusivity. (Diamond level members will later become your key brand ambassadors.) Later, when you are up and running, invite Diamond level members to share a code with friends and family and give them a $25 concession per new member referral on their following year's membership renewal.

## Defining Your Strategic Position: What Business Are You In? Really?

It's not enough to hang a shingle that says "I do concierge medicine." You must say something that is unique and that few others can offer, that makes your customers want to buy from you. What's your elevator pitch?

Your business's strategic position is based on a sustainable competitive advantage based on the following:

| 1. Serving a specific niche in the market |
|---|
| 2. Unique features of your product (membership package) and service (medical care and diagnostic service) |
| 3. Exceptional customer service |
| 4. Price |
| 5. Convenience |
| 6. Something else that distinguishes you from others who offer something similar to your practice (Michael Porter calls this *threat substitution*) |

| *Exit Strategies* | *Your Thoughts* |
|---|---|
| Sell | |
| Be acquired | |
| Merge | |
| Pass on to son, daughter, niece, nephew | |
| Employee buy out | |
| Close and go out of business | |

When you start a business, it has an impact on family and friends. Who will be directly affected? Have you asked for their support, or just assumed you have it? What are their concerns? Do you know? Have you addressed them?

## Review of Chapter 6: Startup Considerations

| What Have You Learned So Far? | |
|---|---|
| 1. Understanding local and state business laws and regulations | |
| 2. Sources of market and competitive research | |
| 3. Business plan development guidance | |
| 4. Computer software and hardware choices | |
| 5. Compliance policies, procedures, and practices | |
| 6. Budgeting and procurement | |
| 7. Marketing, advertising, and public relations | |
| 8. Website and social marketing | |

During this phase, you will have some decisions to make, which are listed in Table 6.2.

**Table 6.2 Key Activities for Phase One[a]**

| *Key Activities in Phase One* | *I Need Help with These Activities* |
|---|---|
| Setting goals for first year | |
| Setting goals for years 2–3 | |
| Setting goals for years 4–5 | |
| Sorting out my priorities | |
| Articulating my business values | |
| Designing my membership offers | |
| Evaluating the Minimum Viable Product | |
| Cost-analyzing the membership inclusions | |
| Setting membership prices | |
| Researching competitors' membership offers | |
| Differentiating my product from competitors | |
| Articulating what makes us unique | |
| Identifying the target market personas | |
| Developing our membership sales strategy | |
| Developing our membership sales scripts | |
| Training a sales coordinator to sell memberships | |
| Finding opportunities in the market | |
| Defining our strategic position | |
| Developing a social media marketing strategy | |
| Executing on a social media marketing strategy | |
| Developing the website framework and function | |
| Developing our website Smart Content | |
| Weighing options for an exit strategy | |
| Researching any local laws I need to know | |
| Help with competitor analysis and opportunities | |
| Help with EHR and MU and other health IT | |

*continued*

**Table 6.2 (continued) Key Activities for Phase One[a]**

| | |
|---|---|
| Help with developing compliance policies, procedures, and documents | |
| Help with budgeting and procurement of technology, mobile health, and personnel | |
| Help with hiring other doctors and clinic staff | |
| Help with marketing advertising and PR strategy | |
| Help with marketing advertising and PR activities and social media campaigns | |

[a] Use the extra spaces above to add to the list, even if it is something unrelated, just so you don't forget it later.

# Chapter 7

# Creating Your Practice Identity

## Creating Your Identity

This is one of the more exciting parts of your business development. I know you are going to be eager to work on this challenging and creative activity as part of your business startup. This is one of the "sticky" activities. It is important that it is well organized, meaningful, and done correctly, because so much of the future is riding on it.

One thing I want to caution you, however: this part can also lead to "analysis paralysis." Don't think that you have to find *just the right name* at this stage. If you are not sure, call it NewCo until you feel more committed to the name. Naming, while important, does not determine your company's future.

Your corporate identity will shape how people recognize your brand, understand the nature of your business, and develop certain feelings (posh, high-cost, hyperbole, accessible, friendly, exacting, trendy, silly, fun, exciting, service-oriented, traditional, and more). These are all influenced by messaging, typestyles, graphics, and the entire brand presentation.

## Your Identity Is Your Brand Image, Not Your Brand

Creating a brand identity can cost thousands of dollars or can be done very reasonably. We have excellent advisors who work with us on our team that bring decades of advertising and branding experience from some of the finest firms, such as Ogilvy, Leo Burnett, Weiden + Kennedy, and others.

Remember the explanation about how consultants work? How they do the first month of nothing but the getting-to-know-you phase?

In order to save money, you may wish to work with a boutique firm that may have these types of specialists available and vetted. Otherwise, for every new consultant, you will need to pay for and go through the fact-finding mission. Branding consultants need this information to begin to build a creative brief. From this, they build a brand standard document. Our experts have created impressive brand standard manuals for our clients. They provide the exact fonts, sizes, logo use in a color setting, a black-and-white setting, how things are worded, corporate standards for brand messaging, and more. We have one client who has agreed to allow its brand standard with some proprietary information redacted, to be used as an example. Contact me if you'd like to see it. It will give you some excellent ideas on what to look for when you engage someone to develop one for you, whether it is your daughter the marketing major and graphic designer whom you hire, or a professional.

One thing that is tough for big agencies to do that we do well is manage small healthcare company accounts with modest budgets, and manage integrated marketing communications. But it's comforting to know that the team members working for you bring decades of agency experience from working with Fortune 100 accounts. Another place you might look for assistance if budget is tight is an intern from a university. You could also contact the professor to see if what you need can be used as a learning lab project by a group of students. Or, you can contact us and we can try to find some students who can help. In lots of communities, the adjunct professors are also willing to do freelance work to supplement their income. Many adjunct professors at colleges and universities don't make enough to get by and are happy to have the work.

Another thing we do is manage digital better than the traditional agencies that are still focused on the world of print advertising, which is very expensive. Not all your advertising and promotion can be Internet based. You will need an integrated strategy that communicates and connects with the market on all channels. Beware of the firms out there who only work search engine optimization (SEO) marketing. They leave a gaping hole in the plan and take all of the budget to aim at a market that may not use the Internet as much as you might assume, or follow different channels from the ones they suggest for you. Generally, your brand image has to be portrayed and identifiable and seen frequently before a buyer will buy. Websites and blogs rarely close sales. People close sales.

## Integrated Marketing Communications

Think of integrated marketing communications like polypharmacy management. For a concierge physician, integrated marketing communications (*integrated marcom*) is trending as more important than a goal of *effective advertising* according to a 2013 *Forbes* magazine survey. An inability to deliver integrated marketing strategies was the reason cited for more agency dismissals and has become a pivotal factor in selecting agencies for campaign pitches. This is especially crucial in the launch of a small boutique concierge medicine practice because your budget is limited and must be spread across an integrated platform. You can't afford an agency that pushes print campaigns or digital only, simply because that's its comfort zone.

## Be Efficient and Run a *Lean* Shop

In your concierge medical practice, you will be the chief marketing officer, even if you delegate the day-to-day activities to a practice manager. Contractors can augment an overwhelmed day-to-day manager with skilled staff who can be assigned to your account, and professional consultants and advisors can be hired to serve as your coach and mentor. In addition to marcom conceptual experts, the contractor can guide the graphic designers and layout artists. The consultant's strength lies in his or her subject matter expertise and domain knowledge in healthcare and concierge medicine development. One who has a cadre of contractors who have been vetted and are familiar with concierge medicine can work faster and more cohesively to create your deliverable by working with talented creative artists who provide the component artwork and layout to round out your needs.

## Finding Unbiased Guidance

When working with a consultant on this part of the startup, be cautious about working with a consultant who has one thing to sell and one way of doing things. For example, a consultant who promotes the direct practice model or the corporate practice (MD VIP and similar brands) and only does those types of conversions, or a physician who converted his or her own practice and is now selling his or her case study as consulting, may not be unbiased. I designed our firm to maintain an unbiased approach to concierge medicine startup and transition. We take no commissions or kickbacks or other incentives (gifts, event tickets, etc.) from the recommended contractors with whom we work. Our position is that we maintain our unbiased position and transparency on everything we recommend. Not all firms work in this manner. Some can charge less because they make it up in referrals and commissions when you choose someone they direct you to, even if that contractor is not the best candidate for the job. Unlike medicine, there is nothing illegal about business consultants who take finder's fees, commissions, and kickbacks. The other campers in our camp may charge more, but the loyalty and duty is to the client. As your coach and mentor, your consultant will provide expert feedback when you have ideas and questions and bring you the benefit of an experienced professional's insight into how to best execute your idea.

## Accountability and Measurement of Marketing ROI

Our maxim is, if you can't measure something, you can't manage it. Marketing accountability is a perfect illustration of that maxim.

You have a right to expect your consultant to be absolutely inflexible and critical about accountability and measurement of your marketing, advertising, public relations, and social media marketing activities. It is simply unacceptable and wasteful as a small company with a tight budget to just throw money at advertising and marketing communications campaigns, market research, and impressions and visibility if the results aren't produced. I am not referring to the one-time $45 ad insertion in the church bulletin. You can do that as often as you like. I am referring to the $2,500-per-month budgets we've encountered being spent by hundreds of medical groups with absolutely no metrics in place to prove any value of continuing the expenditure or strategy. Advertising that doesn't produce business, referrals, or revenue will lead to a quick end to the advertising budget (by depletion) and should also lead to the end of the engagement for an advertising agency or media buyer.

## Web Analytics

Numerous tools exist in the marketplace to perform web analytics and measure your own effectiveness *and that of your competition.*

These tools allow you to gather detailed information about your website including visitor information, SEO details, social statistics, and everything in

**Table 7.1 Key Activities for Phase Two**

| *Key Activities in Phase Two* | *I Need Help with These Activities* |
|---|---|
| Choose a name | |
| Check out trademarks and service marks I want to use | |
| Secure a domain name | |
| Consider logos, taglines, and colors | |
| Choose a graphic designer | |
| Brand positioning advice and field analysis | |
| Integrated marketing communications research and advice | |
| Integrated marketing communications measurement | |
| Integrated marketing communications day-to-day support | |

between from the top sources of data available on the Internet. This is critical for competitive intelligence and brand positioning. When you hire a consultant for assistance with brand positioning, expect the consultant to initially monitor and measure your competition by finding details and measuring Internet analytics on you and your toughest competitors. Then expect him to teach you what you or your staff need to do to continue the monitoring in-house, if you have the time and the commitment for follow through. If you don't think this is important, don't even start the process. Some physicians don't pay attention to their marketing metrics. As I see it, they have not thrived as they could have. They made a choice. There's no judging, remember?

During this phase, you will have some decisions to make, which are listed in Table 7.1.

## *Key Considerations for Choosing a Name*

- If you plan on adding partners or selling the business eventually, you may not want to use your own name.
- If you plan to add a nurse practitioner or physician's assistant (PA) later, you could accidentally create customer expectations that they will always get personal attention from the owner and always be treated by you and no one else.

**COMPANIES LIKE NAMELAB CHARGE BETWEEN $25,000 AND $75,000 FOR AN AVERAGE NAMING PROJECT AND TAKE 4–6 WEEKS TO COMPLETE!**

NameLab's scientific method uses an approach called *constructional linguistics*. The NameLab staff meets with clients to determine what messages a new name should communicate. Then NameLab combs its database of nearly 7,000 morphemes—short, semantic units that when combined form words—to find ones that align with the client's desires. For example, *van* is a morpheme that indicates *front of*, *top of*, or *leading edge*. By combining appropriate morphemes, NameLab generates a long list of candidates, ultimately recommending six to eight names to the client. The majority of the company's creations are neologisms.

- A good company name communicates the correct information.
- A good company name is timeless.
- A good company name is easy to spell and pronounce.
- A good company name is memorable.

## Exercise 1: Business Naming Exercise

| *Questions* | *Name 1* | *Name 2* | *Name 3* |
|---|---|---|---|
| What names have you considered so far? | | | |
| What about the name tells your customers what you do? | | | |
| What about the name tells your customers what they get? | | | |
| What about the name conveys a feeling? What kind of feeling? | | | |
| Are the names already trademarked by someone else? | | | |

| *Questions* | *Name 1* | *Name 2* | *Name 3* |
|---|---|---|---|
| What URLs are available to go with each name? | | | |
| Are there companies with similar or confusing names? | | | |
| Was the name trademarked in a different category? Which one? By whom? | | | |
| Who likes the name and why? | | | |
| Other comments and issues | | | |

## Protecting Your Trademarks and Service Marks

When you acquire a trademark or service mark you get legal protection against others using the mark, name, logo, taglines, and other distinctive marks on competing products or services. You don't own the mark or the name in all instances.

**Have you completed your trademark search with the US Patent and Trademark Office USPTO (http://www.uspto.gov/)?** Secure a domain name that has these characteristics:

1. Identical to your company name
2. Related to the product or service you sell
3. Easy to spell
4. Easy to remember
5. Not likely to be confused with a competitor

**Have you selected a domain name? Consider these issues when choosing logos, taglines, and colors:**

1. A good logo conveys something positive about your company.
2. A good logo has a geometric element that is memorable.
3. It is easy to read, with legible fonts and colors.

**Have you chosen a tagline?**

1. A tagline is used to better explain the nature of the business or create a feeling about your company.
2. Four "beats" approach:
   - "Personalized service at practical prices"
   - "Legal services for the real estate industry"
3. You don't have to choose one now, but it will delay logo design as the two are usually incorporated in the design

**Have you chosen colors for décor, brochures, packaging website, and so on?**

Color psychology considerations: One book I have never let out of my office is *Purpose, Movement, Color: A Strategy for Effective Presentations* by the Mucciolo brothers, Tom and Rich. The book was published in 2003 and is remaindered at many suppliers. You can get it on Amazon.com for less than a dollar these days. The ISBN is 978-0964742802. While it is too old to serve as a good current guide for presentation design, the information contained within it on color psychology is excellent, especially for something that costs less than a dollar!

## Exercise 2: Developing Your Creative Brief

| Business name |
|---|
| Tagline and keywords for marketing material |
| Logo |
| Colors (Pantone matching system [PMS]) |
| Distinct product design |
| Distinct packaging |
| Décor, employee colors, uniforms |

When I consult with clients, I couple this exercise with the business vision worksheets on previous pages so that the designer has something to go by to get started. Graphic designers will help you build the logo and all your stationery and website graphics. They will usually create three–five designs in the initial fee, render them in both color and black-and-white, and render them in all formats for use in print and on the web. They will also convey ownership and copyright for the artwork prepared for you. If they don't include the ownership and copyright, you won't be free to use it as you please.

## Chapter 8

# Getting Organized

Starting a new practice or transitioning an existing one to concierge medicine is a big project. There is far more to the process than simply announcing the grand opening or reopening, and having a membership subscription contract for people to buy what you are selling.

There's much to do and many things to think about. Some of the challenges will be exciting and fun while others, more mundane. Some will be absolute drudgery like setting up budgets, getting business licenses, buying insurance, paying lawyers, etc.

Find a helper so that you don't overlook or underestimate an objective or a task that could cripple your business. Get organized so you stay on track and don't misplace critical information that you'll need in the future.

The tasks for Phase 3 include the following:

| *Tasks* | *I Need Help with These Tasks* |
|---|---|
| Setting up physical files | |
| Setting up digital files | |
| Setting up a contact management system | |
| Keeping track of your company's vital statistics | |
| Keeping track of expenses | |

## Setting Up Physical and Digital Files

The following list is only a start to the files you will eventually need. Feel free to add more as may be relevant to your particular work style and setting.

Accountant
Accounts Payable
Accounts Receivable
Advertising Ideas and Inspiration
Advertising Contracts
Bank Accounts
Customer Contracts
Employee Contracts
Payer Contracts
Customer Leads and Opportunities
Distributors
Entertainment/Meals
Equipment
Ideas and Inspiration for Later
Insurance Policies and Receipts
Investments
Lawyer
Lease
Licenses
Loans
Market Research
- Competitor data
- Competitor brochures
- Demographics data
- Trend data
- Pricing intelligence

Mileage/Parking
Names/Trademarks
Payroll
Staff Training and Development
Suppliers
- EHR Software
- Server security and support
- Practice management software

- Mobile health (mHealth supplier)
- Medical equipment
- Office technology
- Pharmaceuticals and biologicals
- Stationery and printing
- Insurance brokers
- Payroll processing

Tax Matters
Travel (Work-Related)

## Set Up Digital Utilities

1. KeyPass (for passwords)
2. Evernote Web Clipper (for "save it for later")
3. Buffer (for social media posting)
4. Set up Mail Chimp (for newsletter signups)

## Set Up Survey Monkey (for CAHPS Surveys)

Go to https://www.surveymonkey.com/mp/cahps-survey/ and follow the easy-to-implement instructions.

# Chapter 9

# Business Intelligence for the Concierge Medical Practice

Now it is time to start to gather business intelligence about your competitors. Complete the exercises that follow to guide your research. Feel free to add anything that is unique or relevant that goes beyond my checklists.

## Exercise 1: Analysis of Competitors

| **Their Website** | |
|---|---|
| Do they have their own site? | |
| Is it modern looking? Or out of date? | |
| Is it easy to navigate? | |
| Does it contain sticky content? | |
| Does it contain custom graphics and photographs or the same cheesy stock photos on everyone else's site? | |
| Are there patient materials and educational tools present? | |
| Are there downloadable forms? | |
| Can one make an appointment online? | |
| Can one pay a bill online? | |

*continued*

| | |
|---|---|
| Can one download their medical records online? | |
| Does it indicate the insurance plans they accept? | |
| Can one purchase a membership or renew online? | |
| Is the contract downloadable? | |
| Is it private or a franchise? | |
| Do they have testimonials published? | |
| What calls to action do they use? | |
| How large is their staff? | |
| What are their strengths? | |
| What market connections do they have? | |
| How do they position themselves? Self-descriptions | |
| Which segment of the market do they appear to be targeting? | |
| Which websites link to them? | |
| Which competitors have press releases published and about what? | |
| Which keywords are they using? | |
| Are their sites SEO-friendly? | |
| How's their credit? (Dun & Bradstreet ratings can be purchased on anyone.) | |
| Do they position the doctor as an authority on something? | |
| Have they earned citations by industry-relevant domains? | |
| What is the quality/authority of their blog posts, if any? | |
| Are their photos geocoded? | |
| Presence of properly implemented rel = author on website | |

| | |
|---|---|
| Local area code on Local Google Pages | |
| Physical address in city of search | |
| Location keywords in anchor text of inbound links to domain | |
| What is their word-of-mouth approach? | |
| **Offline Advertising** | |
| Which competitors utilize television ads on cable TV? | |
| Which competitors utilize television ads on broadcast TV? | |
| Which competitors advertise in magazines? | |
| Which competitors advertise in in-flight magazines? | |
| Which competitors advertise in local newspapers? | |
| Which competitors advertise in community shopper papers? | |
| **Where can I advertise besides these outlets and my website?** | |
| Concierge Medicine Today | |
| AAPP (American Academy of Private Physicians) | |
| | |
| | |
| | |
| | |
| | |
| **Competitor Social Media Rankings: Positive Sentiment in Reviews** | **My Social Media Rankings: Positive Sentiment in Reviews** |
| HealthGrades Score | HealthGrades Score |
| ZocDoc Score | ZocDoc Score |

*continued*

| | |
|---|---|
| Vitals.com | Vitals.com |
| Yelp | Yelp |
| Twitter followers | Twitter followers |
| Facebook followers | Facebook followers |
| Google+ | Google+ |
| Merchant Circle | Merchant Circle |
| Yahoo listings | Yahoo listings |
| Authority of +1s on website | Authority of +1s on website |
| **SEO Attributes** | **SEO Attributes** |
| Number of shares on Google+ | Number of shares on Google+ |
| Product/service keyword in business title | Product/service keyword in business title |
| Number of circles in which author is contained | Number of circles in which author is contained |
| Matching, public WHOIS information | Matching, public WHOIS information |
| Product/service keyword in website URL | Product/service keyword in website URL |
| **Strategic Partner Potentials** | |
| Welcome Wagon | |
| Branded free pharmacy discount cards (we can supply these to you) | |
| MRI (magnetic resonance imaging) discounts | |
| CT (computed tomography) discounts | |
| PET (positron emission tomography) w/FDG (fluorodeoxyglucose) discounts | |
| Lab testing discounts | |
| Other amenities that don't cost you | |
| Cooperative advertising | |
| Bundled products | |

I don't believe it is necessary to painstakingly explain how this information helps you. It was easier to just show you the list and let you enjoy the epiphanies.

## Public Relations

You can't build your company if you are sitting in your office by yourself. You have to get out in the community, the industry, or both. You should be finding entrepreneurs' clubs and industry associations, making presentations to business groups and local chambers of commerce, and more.

Memberships, meetings, and meals, all of them create opportunities that can't be matched in the virtual world. We'll prepare you to deliver your elevator pitch, and make sure you have professionally designed and quality printed collateral in hand when you go. You just get your wardrobe and shoes in order and accessories that are quality and exude success.

## The Importance of Community

There's no way you can defend that community is irrelevant. For one thing, your concierge practice builds its own community. You are simply the host. Connections to suppliers are built around communities (Craigslist, Angie's List, even eBay).

Many groups will provide you with education you can't pay for. For instance, access Meetup.com for your town or search for groups like these in your area.

- Young Black Professionals new to your town
- Indians and Desis in your town
- Skeptics Society
- Preppers and survivalists
- The Local Wellness Meetup Group
- Local Raw Food Classes
- Local Entrepreneurs and Small Business Marketing
- Local Sophisticated Singles
- Book Clubs
- Garden Clubs
- Mothers of Pre-Schoolers

## The Importance of Associations and Societies

Then there are toastmasters, chambers of commerce, societies, associations, Lions, Kiwanis, Rotary Clubs, churches, journal clubs, etc. Make a list of all the organizations you wish to explore, then make a calendar of events. Find out what it takes to sponsor an event (bring the nachos, pay $10 to introduce the speaker and your business). Be sure to allow enough time to mix and mingle so people can feel free to pull you aside and ask questions. Show off a nifty innovation like the mHealth application that you use in your practice to connect to patients—something they don't get in the traditional mainstream practices.

## Exercise 2: Community Events and Speaking and Public Relations Opportunities

| *Activities* | *I Need Help to Connect with These Activities or Get Bookings* |
|---|---|
| Health fairs | |
| Walk-a-thons | |
| Little League | |
| Host an open house and offer flu shots, BP checks, and more. | |
| Take unassigned ER calls. | |
| Visit pharmacies and leave brochures. | |
| Place brochures with Welcome Wagon, a newcomers club, or a snowbirds club. | |
| Start a medical issue support group for caregivers of that population. | |
| Visit home health equipment stores and leave brochures. | |
| Specialize in difficult conditions and disease and advertise that as a keyword. | |
| Call local employers and offer to come onsite to do physicals, flu shots, wellness talks. | |
| Offer to be a resource for the local media to provide sound bites on the latest health topics. | |
| Send out info to the newspaper every time you attend a meeting, speak, write, or do anything notable. | |

| *Activities* | *I Need Help to Connect with These Activities or Get Bookings* |
|---|---|
| Speak about any medical topic, anytime, anywhere. | |
| Give travel vaccines. | |
| Place a sign outside your practice saying "Now Accepting New Patients." | |
| Meet the local hospitalists group. | |
| Offer virtual visits to your established patients. | |
| Make it incredibly easy for staff from other practices to refer patients to you. | |
| Ask satisfied patients to log in to a physician review site and leave a review of your services. | |
| Visit daycare centers and leave information for parents on kindergarten physicals in the summer. | |
| Develop loss leaders and advertise them: Free/discounted flu shots, inexpensive physicals for those less than 19 years old, etc. | |
| Help students: medical assistants, nurses, phlebotomists, healthcare career students. | |
| Place small ads in the local professional, amateur, or high school theater playbill. | |
| Round twice a day on your inpatients. Satisfied patients refer other patients. | |
| Give a talk at your practice for anyone who thinks he or she might like to be in healthcare. | |
| Moonlight at a local urgent care facility. | |
| Give a talk for local nurses. Everyone asks nurses which doctor they would go to. | |
| Let local (nice) hotels know you will make house calls over lunch or after clinic hours. | |

# Chapter 10

# Startup Red Tape

We've never met a doctor who loved the red tape aspect of starting a new practice. Perhaps you're the first?

## Legal Counsel

Your attorney will play a critical role in this phase of your business startup.

Here are some things to ask the attorney. (Sometimes it is less expensive if you hire a nonlawyer or paralegal do these things and then have the lawyer finalize them.)

| Hiring | I Will Need Help with These Issues |
|---|---|
| Employment contracts—staff (hourly) | |
| Employment contracts—physicians | |
| Employment contracts—managers and supervisors on salary | |
| Overtime and compensatory leave (wage and hour) | |
| Benefits | |
| Nondisclosure/noncompete, employee poaching, trade secrets | |
| Employee handbook | |

| **Compliance Matters** | **I Will Need Help with These Issues** |
|---|---|
| Billing and compliance | |
| Managed care contract disputes | |
| HIPAA (Health Insurance Portability and Accountability Act) and HITECH (Health Information Technology for Economic and Clinical Health Act) security | |
| Credit card acceptance | |
| Employee benefits | |
| Taxes | |
| **Business Organization** | **I Will Need Help with These Issues** |
| Corporate form | |
| Ownership structure | |
| Articles of incorporation | |
| Recordkeeping | |
| Registered agent | |
| Business insurance | |
| Professional insurance | |
| Licensing and permits | |
| Tax Identification numbers | |
| Intellectual property | |
| Trademarks and service marks | |
| Website terms of use /cookies policy | |
| Intellectual property rights and royalties | |

In addition to legal counsel, you may need local assistance with running around to city, state, and other government offices to get permits, licenses, and so forth.

## Exercise 1: Medical Practice Startup Red Tape

| What I Need to Consider | What I Have to Do to Comply |
|---|---|
| Local licenses | |
| Local permits (red bag trash) | |
| County licenses and permits | |
| State licenses | |
| DBA (doing business as) | |
| Federal certifications | |
| FEIN | |
| State employer ID | |
| Business license permit number | |
| Unemployment insurance number | |
| Workers compensation policies | |
| Resellers' licenses (durable goods, vitamins, etc.) | |
| DEA/BNDD (Drug Enforcement Agency/Bureau of Narcotics and Dangerous Drugs) | |
| Occupational licenses | |
| City licenses (if you make house calls or hotel calls) | |
| Business license | |
| Sales tax accounts | |
| Other: | |

# Chapter 11

# Team Building

Aside from dealing with legal issues, you will start building your team in this chapter. Who will be important to your concierge practice success? Who will handle financial affairs, make sales, plan operations, and help you deliver care?

What roles will you fill in-house and what tasks would better be served by being outsourced? To whom should you turn for advice?

Every practice's need for staff is unique. Some practices don't hire anyone and use a professional employer organization, or PEO. That way, the PEO handles all compliance and hiring, benefits management, and recruiting tasks, but you make the final decisions on who gets the job and if and when they are promoted or discharged. Think of it as employee leasing. If you are interested in this approach to human resources management, ask friends and colleagues to point you to some trusted vendors to assist you. You'll recognize some of the names: Wells Fargo, ADP, and others.

Unlike the traditional medical practice, marketing and sales are key roles in the concierge medical practice. In Table 11.1 are a few roles you should consider. Some will not be needed on a full-time basis, while others are difficult to hire on a part-time basis.

## Human Resources Loose Ends

If you choose not to use a PEO, Table 11.2 provides some of the checklist items you'll need to address in order to build a practice handbook.

You will need to develop a Hazardous Substances Plan. Check with the Occupational Safety and Health Administration (OSHA); it has published

**Table 11.1 Team Development**

| *Key Personnel* | *Responsibilities* | *Desired Experience/ Background/Attributes/ Education/Skills/ Target Compensation* |
|---|---|---|
| Top Management | | |
| Nursing/Nursing Assistants | | |
| Financial, Bookkeeping, Accounts Receivable | | |
| Membership Sales Coordination | | |
| Chief Technology Officer, EMR, Internet Compliance and Security, Website development and support | | |
| Marketing, Social Media Coordination, Blogging Editorial Assistant, Public Relations | | |
| Strategic Planning Consultation | | |
| Third-party Payer Contracting, Appeals, Denials, Contracting | | |

standards for these for the lab and other settings that may be helpful. These are available online at osha.gov/.

This is not only good business. ethical, and social responsibility as an employer, but it is critical to protect your brand. So often, concierge physicians advocate and encourage patients to come to their office instead of going to the emergency department at a hospital where the hospital is set up for these kinds of isolation precautions. Don't jeopardize your community respect and brand image by getting caught without this because a patient with a communicable disease comes to your concierge medical practice instead of the emergency department at the hospital.

**Table 11.2 Key Task and Decisions: Team Building**

| *Key Tasks and Decisions* | *I Need Help with These Tasks and Decisions* |
|---|---|
| Work hours and days, overtime, comp time | |
| Vacation days and holiday policies | |
| Sick leave | |
| Personal leave | |
| Bereavement days and jury duty | |
| Hurricane/disaster policy | |
| Employee expense reimbursement policies | |
| Education | |
| Insurance benefits and workers compensation | |
| Retirement program | |
| Training and education: continuing medical education (CME), compliance training | |
| Other benefits (cell phone, auto lease) | |
| Employees and telecommuting | |
| Performance reviews | |
| Recruitment and signing bonuses and policies | |
| Employment agreements | |
| Uniforms and dress codes | |
| Commissions (sales coordinator[s]) | |
| Profit sharing/stock options and vesting policies | |
| Termination policies and disciplinary action plans | |

## Chapter 12

# Operations and Practice Management

Where will you set up your practice? What equipment will you need if you add new service lines? How will you keep track of paperwork? What kind of furniture, fixtures and, equipment (FF&E) will you need? Decisions, decisions, decisions. It's an exciting time in your life. Everything will likely be new or remodeled. It's natural to feel anxious about now. You no doubt have lots of money flying out of the checking account, all of it at risk.

In this chapter I will go over several things, but I won't go over *an introduction to medical practice management.* There are hundreds of books on that topic and none that cover where I am about to take this topic the way I will cover it here. During this phase of your startup, you will deal with issues such as choosing where to work, selecting FF&E, purchasing inventory that could expire if not used on a timely basis, purchasing inventory that could cost more if you buy less than the warehouse stock supply of units. You will also have to deal with the day-to-day mundane aspects that enable you to convert your vision into a functioning business.

## Practice Administration versus Practice Management

Practice administration and management (there is a difference). Simply stated, *administration* has to do with the setting up of objectives and crucial policies of your concierge medical practice. *Management,* by comparison, is the act or function of putting into practice the policies and plans decided upon by the administration. So a practice manager doesn't set your policy, he or she makes it come to life.

Administration (you, or a professionally trained and experienced medical practice administrator) is the top level, whereas management is the middle level of activity. Administration consists of owners who invest the capital and receive the profits from your practice. Managers leverage their specialist skills to fulfill the objectives of the organization. Did the team member you hired to manage your practice fit the former description or the latter?

Managers control and motivate, whereas administrators plan and organize the business functions. This chapter focuses on decisions that are the responsibilities of an administrator, not your practice manager. If you assign them to a manager who doesn't know what they don't know—you will encounter more difficulty than is necessary in the future.

But not every concierge medical practice requires a full-time administrator with a master of business administration (MBA) or master of health administration (MHA)—at least not at the startup stage. Consider purchasing a few hours from an experienced consultant to provide insight, feedback, and guidance in tandem with your accountant and attorney. But by all means, don't abdicate this responsibility to a practice manager who is unprepared to set policy, strategy, and guide your new enterprise to success. Do, however, involve the manager in the steps as needed, so that he or she can give input and execute your policies and strategies to bring your brand to life.

Once you get to that million-dollar practice club—you should then consider putting a professional practice administrator on retainer for a set number of hours each month to act as your mentor and part-time chief strategy officer, because you will be busy. If a doctor called me and said, "Can I hire you to be my part-time practice administrator?," but then spelled out the role she envisaged for me with an expectation that I do "management" (which requires full-time attention), I would have to decline. It isn't the best use of my training and talent, and it isn't the business I am in. For that, I refer them to my colleague and fellow consultant, Mary Pat Whaley, of *Manage My Practice* (http://managemypractice.com). She provides interim or shared, part-time management for physicians. We collaborate; we don't compete.

What seem to be the mundane drudgeries of running a medical practice may make all the difference in whether you are profitable, have sufficient cash flow to pay your bills, or stay out of trouble with regulators. Strategically, the wrong location can doom your practice; a poor quality and safety protocol can result in lower outcomes, waste, and compliance issues. As you work on the design of your concierge medical practice, you should consider developing a detailed operational plan, including a disaster recovery plan, in addition to a marketing plan and overall strategic plan. This is something that has been missing from other concierge medical practice consultants' offers in their proposals. Perhaps they aren't aware of how vital it is or they don't know what goes into such a plan—and they hope you won't call them on it!

## Finding a Location for Your Concierge Medical Practice

How important is your location to the success of your new concierge medical practice? Very important! If you have a business that serves a particular neighborhood or community, you need to be physically located within a drivable distance to service your catchment area, ideally, centered in the catchment area if the demographics align. This business model of medicine is more closely related to retail healthcare than to traditional medical practices that hover around the hospital. That's not to say you shouldn't be close to the hospital, but you don't need to be *in* its medical office building (MOB).

The choice of your facility and neighborhood has an impact on how you and your employees feel about coming to work each day. A pleasant building in a safe neighborhood with ample free parking and ample imaging centers, lab, and medical supply neighbors nearby make for a neighborhood utopian feel and make work more enjoyable. It can also help in recruiting employees.

Our concierge veterinarian operates his practice from the back of his all-wheel-drive Subaru, in true Colorado style. Other concierge physicians I know maintain a house-call and hotel-call practice exclusively. These, too, are offices and require an organizational plan.

In this chapter, I will cover the key considerations for finding and securing your location for your concierge practice. If you are already in a practice and not planning to move, you can skip many of the parts of this chapter that may not apply to you. If you decide to move or expand to a second location, you will find this to be a handy reference checklist.

## Deciding on the Attributes of Your New Concierge Medical Practice Location

Before you begin to search for rented space, start by prioritizing your needs. You may need to call the zoning board and health department to determine any specific requirements to establish a medical practice in your chosen location.

Construction engineers, architects, and medical space planners are specialists, just like some architects specialize in residential or warehouses, or other commercial buildings. You will need to become familiar with some terminology:

**Space plan**—A plan showing how the rooms would be arranged in the space, which would include location of plumbing devices and cabinets.

**Finish schedule** —Items that are necessary for the completion of the architectural drawings, which include selections for hardware, paint, wall coverings, floor coverings, lighting selections, and countertops.

**Leasehold improvements**—Any product attached to the landlord's building including, but not limited to, walls, doors, lighting, cabinets, flooring, plumbing, and ceiling material.

**Shell space**—Space that has no walls, ceilings, lights, or is bare of any improvements.

**Closed bid**—Contractors simultaneously submit their individual construction bids in a sealed envelope, which are subsequently opened by the tenant.

**Construction progress meetings**—Meetings held on a periodic basis that are used to discuss the progress of construction, identify any potential changes, verify schedules and completion times, and so on.

**Punch list**—Items of minor construction that may be completed before or after the tenant takes occupancy.

**Certificate of occupancy**—Before a tenant takes occupancy of an existing or second-generation space and without any construction modification to the space, the city or county often requires the tenant to obtain a certificate of occupancy. At such time, the authority will require the tenant to comply with all existing building code upgrades such as fire alarms; exit signage; emergency lighting; plumbing; parking; and hazardous heating, ventilation, and air conditioning (HVAC) standards and guidelines that are required by the Occupational Health and Safety Administration (OSHA), the National Institute for Occupational Safety and Health (NIOSH), and the local ordinances, etc. Upon such compliance, a tenant will be issued a certificate of occupancy and thus be allowed to occupy the premises.

Before a tenant occupies a newly constructed "shell space," the tenant must not only meet the local building codes, but also meet federal and state codes, such as the Americans with Disabilities Act (ADA) and various state standards. The authority will then issue a certificate of occupancy and the tenant will be allowed to occupy the premises. The staff of the building, if it is a medical office building, will inform you of these codes so they can be incorporated in the planning for your new office. Otherwise, you will need to inquire with an architect, a medical space designer, or other specialist for local ordinances, codes, and design assistance.

During the construction phase, you will probably have a project leader or manager whose goal is to monitor the implementation of the design into construction to ensure that the original intent has not been compromised. Activities occurring during construction that are led by the concierge physician include

- launching internal readiness,
- approving process improvement plans and alignment with evidence-based design (EBD) principles and sustainable practices,
- obtaining zoning and use permits,
- establishing early permit and third-party approvals,
- beginning transition planning, and
- obtaining the certificate of occupancy (CO).

After the construction of your practice is complete, you and your team are moved into the new building or renovated space for a fully operational clinic. You should engage your team members to give input throughout the entire design process, so that they have realistic expectations of working in the new location and maximizing its design features and equipment to improve the transition from old practices under the old brand to the new brand.

Once you are close to your move-in date, you will begin your public relations activities, including

- obtaining feedback from neighborhood leaders,
- performing community outreach, and
- planning marketing activities.

As I work on consulting projects with clinics and hospitals in developing countries, I've been hearing a lot of the phrase "evidence-based design for healthcare" being discussed. Evidence-based design (EBD) is a relatively new field, borrowing terminology and ideas from disciplines such as environmental psychology, architecture, neuroscience, and behavioral economics. Studies have examined (but not really proven) how the physical environment can influence well-being, promote healing, relieve patient pain and stress, and reduce medical errors, infections, and falls. Many hospitals, community health centers, and residential care centers are adopting EBD for new construction, expansion, and remodeling. Be careful that you don't get sold a nice pitch that promises a design package that claims "patient-centered, evidence-based design" without asking some critical questions. You could be paying for a pretty brochure and not much more. EBD is a growing discipline and gaining popularity, and there is an accreditation and certification available to architects and planners (evidence-based design accreditation and certification, or EDAC) from the Center for Health Design. I've been a member of the organization for some time, and on the healthcare section of the American Planning Association and the American Society for Healthcare Engineering, which studies design principles for healthcare buildings. Through these organizations, I am exposed to textiles in the healthcare environment, design and construction, and engineering practices and innovations.

A newly revised standard for ventilation of healthcare facilities can help designers by providing the minimum requirements for the design of ventilation systems for healthcare facilities to provide environmental control for comfort, as well as infection and odor control. The American National Standards Institute (ANSI)/ASHRAE/ASHE Standard 170-2013, *Ventilation of Health Care Facilities*, was written by ASHRAE and the American Society for Healthcare Engineering (ASHE).

Without high-quality ventilation in healthcare facilities, patients, healthcare workers, and visitors can become exposed to contaminants through normal respiration of particles in the air. Ventilation systems and designs for healthcare facilities are intended to provide a comfortable environment for patients, healthcare workers, and visitors while diluting, capturing, and exhausting airborne contaminants including potentially infectious airborne agents. This is one reason why you can't just set up a clinic in any storefront. The revised standard features updates, changes, and clarifications dealing with humidity, ducted returns, recirculating room units, and duct lining. If energy recovery systems are utilized, the systems cannot allow for any cross-contamination of exhaust air back to the supply airstream. Run-around coils are just one example of a system that is permitted. This doesn't mean that your building can't be ecofriendly, but the two standards have to be married by professionals. The standard also addresses some issues that may reduce costs to build and operate healthcare facilities. Standard 170 allows relative humidity as low as 20% for some rooms. This may result in smaller-capacity humidification equipment, lower operating costs, and reduced maintenance costs. The standard permits some use of plenum returns in outpatient facilities, which in turn may result in lower construction costs and operating costs. You can purchase a copy of the standard at http://www.ashrae.org/bookstore. The cost is $58.

You will need to figure out how much space you'll need. One consideration for concierge practices is that you should not need as much space dedicated to a waiting room or reception area. With fewer patients each day and fewer patients scheduled per hour, you may only need one or two seats.

Your activities will be centered on the following clinical services:

- Examination/Treatment Primary Care Clinic Modules
- Specialty Clinics
- Other Patient-Service Programs

Other trends that have been observed within the concierge medicine clinic environment include the following:

**Electronics within the clinic environment:**

- Extensive use of hand-held and portable computers by providers, requiring greater attention to data outlet locations and ergonomics.
- Paperless medical records management systems, resulting in less file storage space needs for future facilities.
- Digital equipment/processing such as radiology and dental, requiring intrasystem software compatibility.
- Telemedical services for expert resource consultation and education. This will continue to advance as a significant movement in medicine tied closely with integrated technology.

**Facility design features:**

- Patient privacy conforming to Health Insurance Portability and Accountability Act (HIPAA) privacy regulations, typically occurring at intake and patient information transfer locations.
- Equipment alcoves adjacent to work areas for medical supplies, weigh stations, crash carts, and other equipment.

- Patient call centers, relieving the provider to focus more directly and efficiently on patient care.
- Patient education centers at waiting areas and central lobbies, in the form of kiosks, brochure displays, and handouts.
- Hands-free infection control operational systems, such as infrared activated lavatory faucets and paper towel dispensers.

Site selection and design are important aspects in the overall success of the concierge medical practice setting. The clinic site should be in a neighborhood with prime commercial or medical office space, or with research, clinical, or technology space that is suitable for medical use. The neighborhood should present a professional image and offer a feeling of security for patients and personnel.

The building site you choose for your concierge practice should accommodate the proposed building and provide the required amount of appropriately located parking with vehicular circulation, loading dock and service vehicle access, emergency vehicle (ambulance) access and entry, safe ways of passage for pedestrians, barrier-free access to public entrances, and adequate open space with landscaping to complement the architecture and create a pleasing outdoor environment.

- Topography should be without steep grades and shall not be affected by the 100-year or 500-year flood plains, rock outcroppings, or adverse subsurface conditions.
- The site should be free of environmental hazards or restrictions.
- The site should provide prominent visibility of the facility from major public thoroughfares.
- Main ingress/egress for on-site pedestrian and vehicular circulation needs to be easily accessible from major public thoroughfares.
- Regularly scheduled public transportation should be conveniently available to the clinic.
- Lighting in the evening should be safe and effective if you plan to invite your concierge membership patients to come to the office instead of the emergency department at night for a quick visit.

## Contemporary Advancements and Evidence-Based Design

Contemporary advancements in healthcare design and practices need to be considered within every design solution, as well as those design features and practices that improve patient confidentiality (HIPAA). Contemporary state-of-the-art design solutions in both private and institutional health facilities should be considered whenever and wherever advancements warrant and can be justified.

This concept of evidence-based design that I referred to earlier offers potential advancements in patient and staff health, safety, and welfare, and should result in demonstrated improvements in outcomes, economic performance, productivity, customer satisfaction, and cultural enlightenment. Evidence-based design components include:

- accessibility/ease of access;
- infection control/operational protocols;
- daylight/natural light potential;
- air quality/natural ventilation;
- noise abatement (possibly utilizing white noise medium);
- application of color, textures, and finishes; and
- environmental/use of artwork, music, and plants.

From a design and building code perspective, business occupancies have much less stringent codes and regulatory requirements than healthcare occupancies. Design and operational issues that are impacted by the healthcare occupancy type include:

- Area (square footage) requirements and accessory support needs
- Procedural protocol accreditation standards (if you plan to pursue accreditation)
- Need for maintaining sterile environment
- Contingencies for patient resuscitation and complications
- Life-safety controls
- HVAC/control system requirements
- Fire protection
- Emergency/critical lighting and power systems
- Disaster planning considerations

I am a little fussy about this area of consideration because I spent several years as a firefighter/EMT and a fire inspector. I became acutely aware of what can happen, and saw many things that could have been avoided with compliance and better planning.

Reception areas support activities necessary to accomplish the tasks associated with medical evaluation and treatment. These include, but are not limited to:

- general waiting areas
- public restroom facilities
- patient educational services (kiosk, education conference room)
- escort/car services
- reception/clerical space

If you know that your style of public relations includes seminars and lectures, you might like to have a training or conference room. The time to investigate that option with your architect and designer is at planning and programming time, so they can wire in the chases for your audiovisual (AV) components and electrical supply, and dimmable lighting. That way, you will always have a place to hold a workshop without having to rent a hall or hotel meeting room or equipment to present your audiovisual material. One orthopedic surgeon I know does concierge arts medicine for performers. He put his extra baby grand Kawai piano in the room for hand surgery patients. When he's not using the room, an ENT (ear, nose, and throat) in the same building who does concierge medicine for vocalists and speakers uses it to work with patients being treated for vocal cord nodes and lesions.

Remember the chapter on market niche? These are market niches in action.

The patient areas accommodate the examination and treatment of all nonemergency outpatients, scheduled and unscheduled.

You can design examination and treatment modules that are generic clinical examination and treatment rooms that accommodate scheduled and unscheduled outpatient visits with variable assignment capability based on schedule and workload needs of the working clinicians. These modules are further subdivided into core space, support space, and specialty clinic space. Spaces within this functional area may include the following:

- reception/waiting space
- public restrooms
- nurse/communication station(s)
- examination/treatment rooms (by module)
- procedure/specialty rooms
- consultation room(s)

- multipurpose room(s)
- provider office space
- clean/soiled utility
- support services (staff restrooms, lockers, lounge)

Patient areas accommodate the examination and treatment of all nonemergency outpatients, scheduled and unscheduled, and inpatients in a variety of medical/surgical disciplines. Examination/treatment modules are generic clinical examination and treatment facilities that accommodate scheduled and unscheduled outpatient visits with variable assignment capability based on schedule and workload needs of the using departments. Modules are further subdivided into core space, support space, and specialty clinic space. Spaces within this functional area may include the following:

- reception/waiting space
- public restrooms
- nurse/communication station(s)
- examination/treatment rooms (by module)
- procedure/specialty rooms
- consultation room(s)
- multipurpose room(s)
- provider office space
- clean/soiled utility
- support services (staff restrooms, lockers, lounge)

## Radiology

You must perform a cost–benefit analysis to determine the feasibility of providing in-house diagnostic radiological services versus contracting for these services in the community or referral to other facilities. Comparisons of availability of services; initial cost of space, equipment, equipment maintenance; and recurring costs of staff, supplies, and utilities should be considered. If in-house diagnostic radiological services are justified, use of teleradiology with transmission of images to a medical center or radiology clinic should be considered to reduce or eliminate the need for an on-site radiologist. A teleradiology setup has been running in the range of $60,000 turnkey through one of my colleagues, a former anesthesiologist and his partner, a radiologist. They set these up at that cost all over the world.

## Laboratory

The basic clinic will provide space (blood draw room, specimen toilet) for collection, labeling, and storage of specimens. Specimens should be transported to a contracted facility for processing. Expanded clinics may include on-site laboratory facilities for limited testing for basic chemistry, hematology, coagulation toxicology, and urinalysis testing most often needed for daily patient monitoring and STAT use. This brings in the Clinical Laboratory Improvement Amendments (CLIA) certification; if the volume warrants, why not approach the lab of choice to rent space from you and place a tech in your office and let them manage that aspect of the practice operations on an outsourced basis?

## Pharmacy/Dispensary

The basic (small) clinic will provide a consultation room for a pharmacist and minimal storage for initial supplies of pharmaceuticals. After providing patient consultation on new prescriptions, the pharmacist will enter prescription data into a designated place on the electronic medical record (EMR). The pharmacist may provide an initial supply of medications to the patient or direct the patient to a contracted pharmacy for medications required immediately. I've studied this option for a number of clients. The burdensome regulations and recordkeeping far outweigh the convenience and market demand for such an arrangement. I don't want to sound polemic, but this is an option I can rarely defend from a business standpoint. But hey, it's your practice.

## Natural Disasters

I grew up in South Florida where hurricanes, tornados, and floods are natural phenomena that occur every year. Then I lived in California where fires and earthquakes were common. Design solutions should address these probabilities where they occur, to mitigate building damage and loss of life wherever possible. Selection of building sites should avoid floodplain or flood-prone areas. Parking lots should be level so people don't have to wade in the water to get to your office. A concierge practice located in areas susceptible to hurricanes should incorporate design features that mitigate damage associated with high winds and wind-driven rain and projectiles. Tornado design mitigation is similar to hurricanes, however much more localized and intensive in nature and often on very short notice. Buildings in areas with probability of earthquakes need to be seismically restrained in accordance with applicable regulations.

## *Floors*

In most clinical spaces, including exam rooms, treatment rooms, corridors, and supply/storage spaces, flooring should be vinyl composition tile with a 4-inch (100-mm) high rubber base. Floors in procedure rooms, surgery, etc. should be welded sheet vinyl with an integral coved base. Floors in offices, conference rooms, and waiting areas should be carpet with a 4-inch (100 mm) high rubber base. Floors in toilet rooms should be ceramic tile with a ceramic tile base. Consider the use of resinous flooring (RES) or wall/ceiling (RES-W) where nonporous seamless surfaces are required/preferred over rigid substrates.

## *Ceilings*

In most clinic spaces, including toilet rooms, we often see lay-in acoustic ceiling tile used. Where required for sanitation or moisture resistance, acoustic ceiling tile should have a washable plastic (mylar) finish.

## *Interior Doors*

Doors should be 1.75 inches (44 mm) thick, solid core, flush wood doors, or hollow metal doors in hollow metal frames. Door jambs should have hospital-type sanitary stops that do not extend to the floor, to facilitate mopping.

Hollow metal doors should be used where high impact is a concern and where fire-rated doors are required. Kick/mop plates should generally be applied to both sides of the doors. Increased door width (42 inches [1050 mm] recommended) is appropriate for extra-wide bariatric wheelchairs.

I've seen clinics fail accreditation inspections because doors were too narrow to accommodate a stretcher in the event an ambulance was summoned to transport a critical patient to the hospital. The landlord didn't want to approve the construction changes to install a wider door, and the surgeon had a 5-year lease, with an in-office operating room and then could not pass accreditation in order to become eligible to care for insured patients in his clinic. All that investment, for not much return.

*Wood doors,* in lieu of steel doors, shall be specified for doors exposed to public view except in humid areas.

## Door Swings

Doors to *housekeeping aids closets* and *isolation rooms* in medical and surgical areas should open out (reverse) and swing 180 degrees wherever possible. Doors to *toilets* should open out (reverse) from the space containing the toilet and should have rescue hardware installed. *Fire-rated* door assemblies, if required, should open in the direction of exit travel and have a fire rating as required by local ordinances. I have seen so many doors installed incorrectly. In cases where a smoke barrier or fire door must remain open under normal conditions (fail safe), select a hardware set that has a magnetic hold-open, or where wall conditions will not allow, a combination closer-holder instead of a closer only. Magnetic hold-opens and closer-holders must be connected to the fire alarm system.

## Safety Glazing

Three types of safety glazing are generally used in interior spaces:

1. *Wire Glass* (W) in steel frames shall be used in the following areas:
   a. Observation windows in fire-rated partitions and smoke partitions.
   b. Vision panels in fire-rated doors and smoke doors.
2. *Laminated Glass* (A) is used as vision panels in doors and observation windows in isolation rooms.
3. *Tempered Glass* (T) is used in all other observation windows and doors with vision panels, including side lights, but is not generally required above doors.

In nonsprinklered buildings requiring fire-rated corridors, all glazing between rooms and corridors is specified to be wire glass in steel frames, subject to size and area limitations of the jurisdiction having lawful authority over the work.

## Stairways

Plan on asking for molded rubber treads on stairs and rubber tile on floor landings and rubber tile on intermediate landings except for stairs exposed to the weather or those in nonpublic areas.

## *Wall Protection at Drinking Fountains and Lavatories*

You should expect the architects to specify solid surface panels on mold-resistant gypsum board on rear walls of drinking fountain alcoves where wallboard or plaster finishes occur and behind lavatories and end walls in exam rooms and treatment rooms that span 30 to 50 inches wide, usually terminating at the nearest inside corner. Solid surfacing generally extends continuously from the top of the wall base to 48 inches minimum above the finished floor.

## *Medical Waste*

Medical waste (the red bags) is generated in exam and treatment spaces where it is bagged, collected, and transported to the soiled utility rooms. There it is held in separate containers pending transport to the medical waste handling facility or disposal by contract. The red bag ownership stays with you even after it is transported and buried in the landfill.

## *General Waste*

General refuse is generated in all spaces and is held in containers for collection and/or sorting.

Disposal is usually by contract. Did you know that there are now garbage concierges that pick up door to door at apartment buildings, so tenants don't have to walk to the trash dumpster?

## *Recycling*

Methods for sorting, collecting, transporting, and disposing of recyclable products must be specifically analyzed for each facility and location. The optional use of disposable and reusable products is an important consideration in recycling and waste disposal alternatives.

## *Soiled Linen*

Soiled reusable linens may be generated in exam rooms, treatment spaces, and patient and staff gowning areas. Soiled linens are collected in carts or hampers (depending on volume) in the soiled utility rooms or soiled linen rooms pending transport to the laundry facility. Disposable linens are included with general recyclable waste or medical waste as appropriate.

## Medical Records

With the increasing popularity of electronic medical records, far less space is now required for storage of medical records. With a concierge practice, you will only need space for about 600 charts. But you will have to store records of the patients who don't follow you to your concierge business in a place for the period of time required by law.

## Space Rental Considerations

Table 12.1 is a list of things to consider when renting space for your concierge practice.

In Table 12.2, you may find it helpful to compare options on one worksheet.

**Table 12.1 Space Rental Considerations**

| | |
|---|---|
| **Cost of rent:** Does your rent require you to pay the taxes, insurance, or even a percentage of your income? Are you required to pay a portion of rent on common areas? | |
| **Length of lease and subletting:** Can you get an option to renew? At what rent? Can you sublet to another physician or a massage therapist or aesthetician or a specialist or another concierge physician some or all of the space? | |
| **Layout:** Does the layout of the space suit your work style or operational needs? | |
| **Leasehold improvements/Remodeling:** Who is responsible for improving the clinic space—you or the landlord? Are you responsible for returning the space back to its original condition when you move? | |
| **Utilities:** What utilities are included in the rent? Are adequate utilities available for electricity, water, and heat? Do you have your own meters or do they bill on a *ratio utility billing system* (RUBS)? | |
| **Janitorial/Maintenance:** Who is responsible for cleaning and repairs? Who is responsible for general and medical waste disposal? | |
| **Zoning laws and other use restrictions:** Are there limits on how you make use of the premises? | |
| **Permits and planning departments:** What kinds of permits will you need to operate your business or remodel? What are the costs and time involved? | |
| **Storage:** Is there adequate storage space for supplies, inactive patient records, and inventory? Is it easily accessible? | |
| **Furniture/Equipment:** Does the space come with any furniture, equipment, or fixtures? If so, are those included in the rent? | |
| **Safety/Security:** Is the location safe for employees, patients, your equipment, and your supplies and drugs? Request a crime occurrence report from the police department for that block, month-over-month, for the past 3 years. | |
| **Expansion:** Is there sufficient space for you to grow? How soon will your needs exceed this space? | |
| **Environmental:** What environmental limitations or concerns apply to this space? Is noise a factor—either noise you produce or noise from the outside? | |

*continued*

**Table 12.1 (continued) Space Rental Considerations**

| | |
|---|---|
| **Insurance:** What insurance does the owner have? What insurance must you provide? Will you have any difficulty getting adequate coverage for this location? | |
| **Access/Parking:** Is the site really accessible for patients, employees, and deliveries? Are there adequate spaces provided for free? Is it near public transportation? | |
| **Appearance:** Will this space make a positive impression for a practice that will be considered up-market? | |
| **Privacy:** Does the space have sufficient privacy for your needs? | |
| **Meeting space/conference rooms:** Does the building have sufficient access to conference rooms and other meeting space? | |
| **Mail shipping and receiving:** Can you receive shipments there? Is it secure? What time do shipments arrive and what time are they picked up? | |
| **Coffee/kitchen/eating areas:** Is there access to any coffee, food preparation, or eating areas? Is water convenient? | |
| **Lighting:** Does the space have adequate natural light to avoid eye strain and eye fatigue? | |
| **Wiring/Data lines:** Is the space already wired for high-speed Internet access? If not, will it be difficult or expensive to install? | |
| **Fellow tenants/Neighbors:** Are the neighbors compatible with similar market demographics? | |
| **Limitations on space, additional fees:** Are there any limits on your hours of operation or requirements to pay additional fees or participate in certain activities, for example, if you want to use the conference room on a Saturday for a health fair of your own? | |

**Table 12.2 Worksheet: Location/Space Comparison Chart**

| | *Location One* | *Location Two* | *Location Three* |
|---|---|---|---|
| Address | | | |
| Contact info | | | |
| Total square feet | | | |
| Rent (per square foot, total) | | | |
| Length of lease | | | |
| What is included? | | | |
| What are you responsible for? | | | |
| Legal and zoning issues | | | |
| Parking access and safety issues | | | |
| Insurance issues | | | |
| Advantages | | | |
| Disadvantages | | | |
| Other | | | |

# Chapter 13

# Designing the Layout of Your New Concierge Practice

The point in the timeline between finding your location and moving in is where you begin to design the layout for how you will use your space. We will complete several worksheets based on the information you develop in the rest of this chapter. These are the same worksheets I might leave with a physician at the initial on-site consultation when I am aware that there will be a space redesign for the client.

Work with a list to standardize your medical supplies and equipment, based on the preventive care, diagnostic testing, and treatments you plan to offer in your practice. These standard lists will help you make better, easier, and faster choices of medical supplies and equipment, which will help you improve patient care, contain costs, and spend less time on procurement activities. They also help in the event you want to become accredited by the Joint Commission or another accrediting body that surveys physician practices and outpatient clinics.

Another benefit of these lists is that you will have a framework for budgeting, and you will avoid impulse expenditures of items that are rarely or never used. You will also reduce duplication of items used for the same purpose. The use of a good up-to-date list will also help you prioritize new acquisitions of testing equipment and supplies.

By using a standard list, you will also improve supply chain management because you will reduce the number of items that need to be supplied. You can divide the supplies into categories, including:

- Vital
- Essential
- Never (occasional use)

This *VEN* system will help identify the things that should always be on hand. By encouraging uniformity, you will also safeguard against pilferage, and simplify stock control, ordering, and preventive maintenance (like checking the freshness of the "C" batteries on the crash cart, for example). These lists can also provide the basis for standard maintenance training for your patient care staff, including nurses and technicians. You will also begin to better manage the range of spare parts, accessories, and consumables required, which simplifies sourcing. It will also help you decide to take advantage of any bargains and combination packages that dealers tend to offer from time to time. Supplies that are close to their expiration date are sometimes offered for sale at low prices. Be careful not to buy more than you can use before the expiration date, otherwise you will waste resources. Packaging also adds to the cost of supplies and equipment, but it is usually worthwhile to purchase goods that are well packaged. Poorly packaged goods are more likely to be damaged in transit.

Better quality supplies and equipment are more expensive, but cheaper supplies and equipment are often of poor quality. Buying the cheapest items can be a false economy because they may need repairing or replacing more frequently. It may be more cost effective to spend more on a higher-quality item that is more reliable and that lasts longer. I've put my hands right through cheap gloves that were purchased on "closeout." They wouldn't even hold the air when blown up as a balloon!

It is beyond the scope of this book to include everything you need to know to start and run a concierge medical practice, so it really doesn't provide all the information on nonmedical and communications equipment, furnishings, stationery, etc.

In these next exercises, you will take time to review the skills and competence of your workforce, the medical services you plan to make available to patients, the amenities you plan to offer as part of your concierge membership product, and how you plan to organize your production and back-office areas.

These lists and worksheets are inanimate. They won't update themselves. You and your staff must review your lists on a regular basis, and when there's downtime in the office, obtain current prices from suppliers. Better yet, hand the list to the several competing suppliers and have them prepare custom order sheets for you with the prices listed next to the item. Ask them to update the lists for you every 3 months. You can remind yourself to do this by setting it as a recurring calendar item in your online calendar, which should send you an email or SMS (Short Message Service) reminder.

The trade-off: The suppliers benefit by being able to gather excellent business intelligence by having an idea of what you need, how often you reorder, and where they are not competitive if you are not ordering from them. You save time and have the facts on hand to be a better and more frugal shopper.

If you decide to seek Joint Commission accreditation or the DNV Healthcare Inc. National Integrated Accreditation of Healthcare Organizations (NIAHO) accreditation, you may wish to incorporate these lists and procurement standards, which benchmark the quality of the items you purchase to globally recognized safety and performance standards. Since readers of this book are international, I've included some of the international standards (not just American standards) in Figure 13.1.

All medical supplies and equipment should meet international, regional, or national safety and performance standards. The most important standards include:

- IEC – which are international standards for the electrical safety of electrical and electromechanical equipment, and apply to refrigerators, for example. IEC 601 is the international standard specifically for electrical and mechanically safe medical equipment for use by staff and with patients.
- ISO – which are international standards for quality management and systems. ISO 9000–9004 is a series of standards covering the quality of manufacturing processes, design and development, construction, installation, and service. ISO standards do not currently exist for all medical supplies and equipment, but they do apply to syringes, needles, gloves, instruments, and scales, for example.
- CE mark – which indicates that a product meets European Union directive standards, and applies to sterile medical supplies, for example.
- Pharmacopoeia specifications – which establish quality specifications for the most commonly used drugs and some medical supplies, such as bandages, tape, and swabs. Important pharmacopoeias include the British (BP), European (EP), United States (USP), and WHO International Pharmacopoeia (IP).
- Quality certificates or export certificates – which are issued under various national and regional standards such as ISO 9000 or the equivalent EN 29000.

**Figure 13.1 Safety and performance standards for medical equipment and supplies.**

If possible, before purchasing, check the quality of the labeling and the packaging. Labeling should include information about country of origin, date of manufacture and, if appropriate, expiry date and storage instructions.

Packaging should protect supplies and equipment from damage or deterioration during transit and storage. Labeling or packaging also includes information that manufacturers are required to provide to users. This information is sometimes presented as symbols, which are intended to be understood by any user irrespective of native language.

Another important factor is the source of supplies and equipment. There are issues to consider related to

- manufacturers and suppliers,
- imported supplies, and
- used supplies.

The quality of manufacturing standards differs from country to country. Only procure supplies and equipment from a licensed, reputable, and reliable source. Before buying, ask the supplier which safety and performance standards an item complies with. Be wary of copies—items made to look like a well-known brand—as these are often of poor quality and do not conform to international standards. I have organized many purchases of slightly used equipment for clients through DOT.med (http://dotmed.com) and Craigslist (http://craigslist.org), and even eBay (http://ebay.com) from time to time. I have also helped liquidate used equipment for clients on these sites. One Mexican hospital was able to quickly (3 days) sell a used 1.5 Tesla MRI (magnetic resonance imaging) and 4-slice CT (computed tomography) scanner in a week going through DOT.med, and then found a bargain on a newer model for thousands of dollars less. It just wasn't the latest or greatest, but it was functional and affordable.

If you decide to purchase used, refurbished, or reconditioned equipment, Table 13.1 may help you decide more easily.

Sometimes it is more cost effective to buy new rather than used equipment, which only has a limited life. Obtaining accessories, consumables, and spare parts can also be difficult for older models that are no longer made. Find out the cost of a new model of the same or a similar item of equipment and compare this with the cost of the used model. Once you decide to retire a piece of equipment, have a process in place to take it off the books (accounting procedures) and dispose of it properly. If there is metal or

**Table 13.1 Used/Refurbished Equipment Purchasing Worksheet**

| | *YES* | *NO* |
|---|---|---|
| 1. What condition is the equipment in? | | |
| 2. How much longer will it last? | | |
| 3. If it has been reconditioned, what is its new lifetime? | | |
| 4. Will it be supplied with installation and use instructions and service and repair manuals? | | |
| 5. Has it been fully tested and calibrated? | | |
| 6. Are all the essential parts, and at least a 2-year supply of accessories and working materials (including all the consumables and spare parts needed to use the equipment) included? | | |
| 7. Will the supplier be able to continue to provide accessories, consumables and spare parts, technical support and maintenance for the future life of the item? | | |
| 8. What after-sales support will the supplier provide? | | |
| 9. How long will it take from placing the order to receiving the item? | | |
| 10. Will staff have to be trained to use the equipment or are they already familiar with it? | | |

copper, consider recycling. If it is really old, donate it to a medical museum, like the A.T. Still University Museum of Osteopathic Medicine.

If you are thinking about importing supplies and equipment, you will need a foreign procurement vendor or exchange. Find out if the supplier will provide all the necessary documentation for customs clearance and decide whether you can deal with import procedures, transport, insurance, and other arrangements. I've known many physicians who travel internationally and bring home souvenirs in the form of interesting or advanced medical technology from abroad. Be careful to review your professional liability policy to ensure that you are covered when using technologies that may not be proven effective and safe by the U.S. Food and Drug Administration (FDA), if used in the United States, or by your medical commissioning authority in your country.

Another point to consider is staff competency to use and maintain the supplies and equipment you purchase. What is the point of obtaining items if your staff doesn't have the expertise or training to use them properly or if you cannot access maintenance and technical support? I've run into this situation in Nigeria, South America, and Kansas.

Accreditation standards require that you must be able to obtain service on equipment within a specified time frame (generally 4 hours or less). The standards also require that you record the competency testing, standards, and criteria to measure competency with each piece of equipment for each staff member. Whether or not you choose to become accredited, or you just bill Medicare and insurers for your services, these requirements are in the various managed care plan administrative manuals, the conditions of participation, standards of care, standards for storage, handling, dispensation, and administration of drugs and biological, standards and procedures for reporting adverse reactions to a treatment, or equipment error or malfunction. The Institute of Medicine (IOM) calls for competency-based criteria to evaluate knowledge, skills, and abilities for emerging and traditional care. Many product manufacturers now offer, as a competitive advantage, American Nurses Credentialing Center (ANCC)-accredited skills competency programs with their medical technology and equipment leases and sales.

## Exercise 1: Practice Layout Consideration

First, ask yourself the following questions:

1. What are the necessary functions you will perform in the office?
    - Acupuncture
    - Aesthetics
    - BMI calculations
    - Catheter changes
    - CIMT
    - Clinical trials
    - Crash cart
    - Digital scale
    - Echocardiography
    - EKG
    - Hearing tests
    - Immunizations and trigger point injections
    - Intubation and cricothyrotomy kit
    - Laceration repairs
    - Limited lab

- Massage
- Mechanical beam scale
- mHealth consultations
- Nutritional counseling
- Pap smears and pelvic exams
- Patient visits
- PICC lines placement
- Plethysmography
- PRP processing
- Psychotherapy
- Pulse oximetry
- RAST testing
- Reception
- Spirometry
- Stem cell preparation
- Urinalysis
- Vision tests
- X-ray

2. Are there other locations besides the office where functions happen?
    - Billing
    - Collections
    - Accounting
    - Payroll
    - Human Resources
    - Home diagnostics—the Internet of Things—all the smart devices that now connect to you, whether your fridge or your fitness wristband

3. How will you divide the available functional space between different functions?

4. How many employees will be working in each area of your space?
    a. At grand opening
    b. In 6 months
    c. In 12 months
    d. In 3 years
    e. In 5 years

*continued*

| 5. Will you have employees working in an open environment or cubicles? |
|---|
| 6. Do some employees need private offices?<br>Space permitting, I would always place sales coordinators in a private office with a door that closes, not just an alcove or a desk in the lobby. You want your new members to feel that they are being treated with the utmost respect and afforded the highest quality in service. Your office manager should also have a private desk that fits at least two guest chairs and shelf space to put all the manuals and management tools they need. |
| 7. How much equipment will you have and how large is it? |
| 8. What noise is generated by the equipment? |

## Exercise 2: Floor Plan Layout

Use the grid for planning your office (treatment, storage, reception area). Determine an equivalent for each square on the grid. Otherwise, use graph paper available from any office supply store.

## Exercise 3: Designing Your Operations Processes and Evaluating Your Costs

As you outline the steps involved in a typical office visit and the procedures you will perform in your office, consider the following items: how long each step will take, who is involved, who will be responsible, and so forth. Use one worksheet per activity (IOV, ROV, EKG, PFT, etc.). When you are done, place them in your notebook.

**Note:** So often, I listen to the "sellers' remorse" of concierge physicians who set membership amenities and service inclusions in their package without knowing the cost of those inclusions. Then, 24 to 36 months into their operations, they complain that their contract with the members stipulates to certain inclusions, and they cannot cancel or modify those services without causing a lot of grief about contract amendments. They expect that any reduction would be met with an expectation of a lowered membership fee, when in essence they priced their program recklessly. In fact, a competitor could file an antitrust complaint for predatory pricing.*

| ACTIVITY—CPT CODE: | |
|---|---|
| What supplies do I need? | |
| From whom will I procure them? | |
| What is the price range at which I can easily procure them? | |
| When do I need them? | |
| How long do they remain fresh or usable? | |
| How much labor is required? | |
| What is the labor cost? | |
| What is the activity-based cost of this activity? | |
| What margin do I hope to realize? | |
| What price or value is assigned to this activity? | |

*continued*

* The pricing of goods or services at such a low level that other suppliers cannot compete and are forced to leave the market.

| | |
|---|---|
| How will I set standards or where will I borrow the standards that are already accepted in the industry? | |
| How will I reduce inefficiencies in the process? | |
| How will I ensure worker safety? | |
| How will I ensure patient safety? | |
| How can I reduce waste? | |
| How will I dispose of waste? | |
| Additional considerations: | |
| | |
| | |
| | |
| | |

A few more things to consider before we leave this train of thought:

1. How large a reception area will you need for a practice that runs on time and sees fewer patients per hour?
2. Will you require a separate check-in and check-out desk?
3. How will you provide space for a coffee area, kitchen, or other break room needs?
4. How much space is needed for storage and where is it best located?

Don't forget to provide space for all the usual business support equipment:

- Copying
- Faxing
- Mail preparation
- Bathrooms for patients
- Bathrooms for staff
- Teleconferencing with patients

Even if you hire a medical interior decorator or ergonomics specialist to help you with your floor plan, you will save money if you have your ideas worked out and measurements taken before meeting with them.

# Chapter 14

# Planning the Move to Your New Concierge Medical Practice Location

Here's a story about planning the commissioning of new buildings and offices and why you should *give a little thought* to how you will execute the move to your new digs.

The Rocky Flats Plant was a United States nuclear weapons production facility near Denver, Colorado, that operated from 1952 to 1992. It was under the control of the United States Atomic Energy Commission (AEC) until 1977, when the AEC was replaced by the Department of Energy (DOE). Weapons production ended in 1989 after FBI agents raided the Rocky Flats Plant. Rockwell International, the operators of the plant, later pleaded guilty to criminal violations of environmental law. But it didn't end there.

Rockwell International was replaced by EG&G, formally known as Edgerton, Germeshausen, and Grier, Inc., as primary contractor for the Rocky Flats Plant. Around 1997, then Energy Secretary Federico Peña was scheduled to visit the huge plant to designate its closure plan, which would then be delivered to the president in 1998. The last contaminated building was removed and the last weapons-grade plutonium was shipped out in 2003, ending the cleanup based on a modified cleanup agreement. With all the planning and logistics, one would expect that someone could have been held accountable to order and supervise the installation of the carpet in the huge reception area at Rocky Flats prior to when Mr. Peña was slated to arrive. Nope. The carpet (and padding) had to be ordered and delivered by FedEx Custom Critical on a Sunday so that it could be installed prior to his arrival. It troubles me that they had to go to such great expense to welcome someone who was delivering their death sentence and closure order within 6 years' time, since commercial grade carpet is supposed to have a 5- to 10-year normal wear life. I've been unable to find the exact dollar amount that was paid, though I know it is contained in declassified information about the site, and it will poke up some day in a museum, I am sure.

So how much will you waste on poor planning for your office move in? Hopefully you won't waste anything. Table 14.1 is a checklist you can use to start planning your move to the new office location.

When you go shopping for office furniture, there are lots of places to choose from that can save you money over the retail big box stores. Use the retail establishments to shop makes and models and touch and see quality, textures, and fabrics. Err to the side of less is more for an elegant and sophisticated concierge medical practice. Purchase quality that lasts instead of less expensive throwaway merchandise.

Table 14.2 is a checklist you can use to track purchases and compare prices and models while doing prepurchase reconnaissance.

## Should You Purchase or Lease?

As a rule, most people purchase the less expensive items and lease more costly ones. Try not to tie up cash unnecessarily. If you are uncertain that you will succeed in concierge medicine, opt for short-term leases on your equipment. Even if this means higher monthly payments, in the short run, you buy your flexibility to get out of your lease if conditions change.

Always ask your accountant about tax implications of leasing versus buying: some deductions can make leasing actually cost less than buying.

Finally, don't buy more than you need. Cash in the bank beats a nice desk chair every day of the week.

**Table 14.1 Checklist for Physician Practice Move**

| *Checklist for Practice Move* | | *Assigned to* | *Completed?* |
|---|---|---|---|
| After you have received your certificate of occupancy, and all construction is near completion, you can begin most of these plans. | | | |
| *Lead Time* | *Activity* | | |
| **12 Weeks** | **Moving Company:** | | |
| | Interview several companies and get estimates. | | |
| | Are they experienced in moving sensitive equipment? | | |
| | Are they available when you need them? | | |
| | Evaluation of all high-priced equipment (medical equipment, computers, phones, etc.) Should be moved by specialized movers | | |
| | Confirm/arrange for the new location to have high-speed Internet access for billing, data transmission, etc.; contact phone service supplier. | | |
| **12 Weeks** | **Telephone:** | | |
| | Plan to switch over phones on least busy day of the week. | | |
| **12 Weeks** | **Answering Service:** | | |
| | Coordinate with telephone service changes. | | |
| **12 Weeks** | **Payors:** | | |
| | Medicare | | |
| | Medicaid | | |
| | Contracts (HMO, PPO)<br>*Note:* Check notice and location requirements because some companies will only continue your contract if they approve the location. If you change counties, or enter a zone that has been contracted exclusively with another provider, you may be in for a nasty surprise. | | |

*continued*

**Table 14.1 (continued) Checklist for Physician Practice Move**

| *Checklist for Practice Move* | | *Assigned to* | *Completed?* |
|---|---|---|---|
| *Lead Time* | *Activity* | | |
| | Commercial Carriers | | |
| | Other | | |
| **8 Weeks** | **Printed Materials: Place Order** | | |
| | Appointment cards | | |
| | Brochures | | |
| | Checks, deposit slips | | |
| | Prescription pads | | |
| | Stationery, envelopes | | |
| | Other | | |
| **8 Weeks** | **Contract computer vendor about move, new location, etc.** | | |
| **8 Weeks** | **Periodicals** | | |
| | Other subscriptions | | |
| | Medical associations | | |
| **4 Weeks** | **Notify P&C Insurance Carriers:** | | |
| | Health/Dental policies | | |
| | Malpractice policies | | |
| | Office/Business policies | | |
| **4 Weeks** | **Notify Equipment and Supplies:** | | |
| | Maintenance contracts | | |
| | Suppliers (business) | | |
| | Suppliers (medical) | | |
| **4 Weeks** | **Contact Outside Services:** | | |
| | Biohazard removal services | | |
| | Janitorial service | | |
| | Payroll service | | |
| | Postage meter | | |

**Table 14.1 (continued) Checklist for Physician Practice Move**

| *Checklist for Practice Move* | | *Assigned to* | *Completed?* |
|---|---|---|---|
| *Lead Time* | *Activity* | | |
| **4 Weeks** | **Contact All Referral Sources:** | | |
| | Ancillary referrals | | |
| | Office managers | | |
| | Physicians | | |
| | Other | | |
| **4 Weeks** | **Notify Professional Services (by mail):** | | |
| | Accountant | | |
| | Attorney | | |
| | Banker | | |
| | Consultant | | |
| **2 Weeks** | **Arrange Change of Address for Each Physician:** | | |
| | DEA License | | |
| | State license to medical board | | |
| | Occupational license | | |
| | Sales tax registration, etc. | | |
| **2 Weeks** | **Post Office** | | |
| | Notification, forwarding, holding of mail | | |
| **1 Week** | **Hospital Medical Staff Office** | | |

**Notes:**

1. Allow time to test and recalibrate equipment and systems.
2. When confirming appointments, notify patients of new office location.
3. When scheduling patients, notify them of new office location.
4. As patients check out and reschedule, inform them of the new office location.
5. Place signs redirecting patients to new location. Update maps and website links.

**TABLE 14.2 Furniture Shopping List**

| *Furniture* | *Quantity* | *Cost per Item* | *Vendor* | *Date Ordered* | *Delivery Date* |
|---|---|---|---|---|---|
| Desk | | | | | |
| Desk chair | | | | | |
| Reception desk | | | | | |
| Guest chairs | | | | | |
| Exam tables | | | | | |
| Conference room table | | | | | |
| Book and storage shelves/cabinets | | | | | |
| Filing cabinets | | | | | |
| Lamps and lighting | | | | | |
| Fire safe, secure storage | | | | | |
| Whiteboards | | | | | |
| Cubicle frames and dividers | | | | | |
| Rugs | | | | | |
| Decorative art | | | | | |
| Mirrors | | | | | |
| Other: | | | | | |

## Exercise 1: Warranties and Service Contracts to Manage

Start a spreadsheet on your computer and begin with two columns and nine rows. In Column A, list the following in rows:

- Equipment
- Make
- Model
- Serial Number
- Place Purchased
- Telephone Number of Customer Service
- Warranty Terms
- Expiration Date
- Notes

**Table 14.3 Questions to Ask a Potential Medical Goods or Technology Supplier**

| **Questions to ask a potential supplier:** | |
|---|---|
| Name of supplier | |
| Representative's name | |
| Representative's phone/email/SMS | |
| Types of products or services | |
| How long has the firm been in business? | |
| What other customers do you serve in the building? | |
| What is your usual turn-around time on orders? | |
| What is the quickest time possible in special circumstances? | |
| What payment terms do you offer? | |
| How large a credit line will you extend to me? | |
| Can you meet special packing or shipping requirements? | |
| Do you have minimum order requirements? | |
| Are discounts available? | |
| Other: | |

In Column B leave enough room to complete the information.

Don't always opt for extended warranties on items that cost less than $1000.

In Table 14.3, I've included a checklist for your use to vet suppliers before doing business with those you may not know well.

## Business Technology Purchases

We all love technology—when it works. I can't imagine my life without technology—especially my Nespresso cappuccino maker. It makes coffee perfectly when I am functionally impaired every morning. As long as I can press a button, I am good to go.

Technology drastically lowers the cost of doing business by performing many business functions for us. This next worksheet will help you outline your business technology needs.

Start by establishing a technology strategy. In big companies and hospitals, they have chief technology officers (CTOs). Guess what? You're it.

I counsel clients to make technology purchases with a little room to grow—2 to 3 years. At that point, what you will have will be functional; not the latest and greatest. Don't buy the lower-end model that is about to be discontinued.

First, research what you absolutely have to have. This is like an exercise in Maslow's hierarchy of needs—needs become wants. Sort it out.

Next, decide if your needs are basic or complex. For complex needs and software, I sometimes figure I can go to a place like Kinko's FedEx if it is a one-off need, rather than make a purchase.

Following this, determine if you need interoperability with other equipment.

Next, determine if you need single-purpose or multifunction equipment. Don't be fooled by nearly free printers and such and then have to pay a fortune for special supplies.

## Business Communications Purchases

Your telephone is your single most important piece of equipment; like a lifeline to the world. In this day and age, it is not surprising to see physicians with two cell phones. Better than have to carry two phones, get one phone with two lines. I have three of them. They carry dual SIM cards and I keep one for my T-Mobile account, and one into which I pop international SIMs when I travel the world. That way, clients can find me if I am not flying or otherwise unavailable, like standing in an OR.

Beyond this, I am not going to assume you don't know how to purchase a cell phone in this day and age.

## Software and Hardware Purchases

Purchasing a computer system for your practice can be time consuming and daunting. I got ready to write this section and searched Google. I used "purchasing physician computer system" as my search phrase and came up with more than 14 million results. I am not the expert in this. Call someone who is your expert, not a vendor rep or someone who gets a kickback or finder's fee for sending you in their direction.

I like Practice Fusion for free EHR (electronic health records). I've installed it and had it up and running in Mexico, the United States, Nigeria, Germany, and Colombia.

During my search, I came upon an article in the American College of Physicians' ACP Internist®. It was hysterically funny (http://www.acpinternist.org/archives/1995/05/tipskatz.htm). What was even funnier was that it came up at the top of the search. It was written in 1995 and was summarized as a "no nonsense guide to buying computer hardware." Where is Dr. Carter now? He wrote a book on EHR implementation that is in its second edition.

You are also going to need to choose an Internet service provider (ISP). Typically, the ISP provides you with access to the Internet and email. But if you are smart, you won't use your ISP's email address except for behind the scenes. It is likely you will purchase a domain name for your website. The domain name is the actual name of the website, such as www.drsmith.com, while a URL may be any one of the pages within the domain such as http://drsmith.com/medical or http://drsmith/contactme and so on.

Earlier in the book, I reviewed how to reserve your domain name. Once you have that, you can use it for your email address. You will be able to use your domain name with almost any ISP. I go absolutely nuts when I hear doctors tell me that they bought it from GoDaddy, so they thought that they had to get their email from GoDaddy and host their website with GoDaddy. You will need a dedicated server for a medical practice, not one of the inexpensive slow versions that put you on the same shared server with three XXX-rated websites!

All of these issues must also be reviewed by your Health Insurance Portability and Accountability Act (HIPAA) and Health Information Technology for Economic and Clinical Health Act (HITECH) compliance technicians.

Most likely, you will need a technology consultant. I am lucky; my husband is a competent and qualified technology guy. He helps me when my back is against the wall, but I also have professional hired help and have learned to help myself. Here are some lessons learned: Once in 2002, the medical group I worked with to prepare for HIPAA hired a tech guy they found from a guy who knew a guy. He seemed competent, and the doctors were dead set on hiring this guy because he came highly recommended. He talked a good game, had a relatively new Volvo, lived in Santa Monica—I think (we could never find him). His price was a little high, but the doctors wanted the job done right, so they were ready to pay a little more than market rate. We became cordial, and then I had trouble with my little personal Sony Vaio. The Vaio was out of warranty. My husband was back in Las Vegas and I was in California. I asked this consultant to take a peek. He had just been paid the second tranche installment for his work, and still had one third to go. He asked if he could take it home overnight. I acquiesced, and never saw my little Sony Vaio again. It was a good thing that it had no HIPAA information on it. I tried to serve him with a lawsuit to get my property back, I filed a police report, and I sent the process server to the address on the contract for the office. It was an abandoned building, not a home or office. We never saw him again. I had to find a new technology consultant to help with the HIPAA completion and testing. In 2002, that was a $30,000 contract. In today's dollars that's over $38,000.

If you can find reliable consultants, use them—especially when you are just getting started. Ask for recommendations, and remember, recommendations are highly biased sometimes—kind of like restaurant recommendations. Some people like Burger King and McDonald's. I go there for coffee or a soda. I buy hamburgers from the butcher, who grinds them. We don't eat burgers outside the house. When you pick a technology consultant, part of what you are paying for is translation to English. Make sure they speak more than technology lingo.

You will need a technology plan that incorporates how the hardware and software will work together to achieve your goals and objectives. These days, I visit practices that have buyers' remorse on many packages. Drive your decisions on the basis of functionality and let a technician pull that together. Don't get suckered into buying bundles of things you don't need. If you plan to join an accountable care organization (ACO), you have to play well with others, too.

Practice management (PM) software runs the business side of healthcare, from scheduling patients, to billing, to generating monthly reports, so picking the right system is crucial for any size medical practice. Unlike with electronic health records (EHRs), selecting and overseeing a PM system isn't typically the physician's domain in large practices like the ones that the Medical Group Management Association (MGMA) advises. They have the market for groups that are 10 doctors or more. The Professional Association of Health Care Office Management (PAHCOM) caters to the 10 and fewer physician practice size. The American Academy of Private Physicians (AAPP) is supposedly the nonprofit trade association of concierge physicians, but I don't see any of the three of these organizations really meeting the needs of its members in this specific area. I see sponsors for their conference, but I don't see helpful articles on their websites about things that doctors need. Are they all just conference companies now?

# Chapter 15

# Money Matters

In this chapter we talk about spending money, tracking expenses, setting budgets, banking, and all that wonderful stuff.

Everyone brings *issues* to this chapter. Most of you have lots of school debt and money is a topic that is very personal. Most every physician I know tends to want to skip over the topic of budgets, bookkeeping, and accounting. Even if you enjoyed math class, this is drudgery for most. By the time clients get to me to convert or develop a concierge medical practice for them, they've already got a relationship with an accountant who is a family friend, relative, or mentor.

Money matters for physicians is something you have to learn to manage like bad-tasting medicine. Open the hatch, drop it in, make the face, and move forward. Financial reports are no reflection of your character—no matter if they are red ink (loss) or black ink (profit). They just are what they are. You will have to learn how to discuss a raise with an employee without feeling you are being challenged, and stand and deliver when it's time to tell a client about the price of your services.

It is critical that you learn how to manage money for your business and personal life. Did you know you can be profitable and still not have enough cash on hand to pay your bills on time? You have to understand about cash flow and setting up financial procedures from the start of your new business.

This chapter starts by having you select an accountant to work with. They will help you with your accounting procedures, bookkeeping, and benefits and taxes. They prove their value when they help you legitimately lower your tax burden and show you how to optimize that which you work so hard to earn.

Here are the questions you need to ask your accountant:

- What kinds of taxes will I have to pay?
- When are the deadlines?
- How can I reduce my taxes appropriately?
- Which expenses are deductible?
- How can I prevent embezzlement?
- How should I pay myself in the beginning? Will it change?
- Should I use the cash method of accounting or accrual?
- How do I keep track of inventory I sell, if any?
- How should I handle payroll taxes?
- Do I have to collect state tax? If yes, from whom?
- What if I do business in more than one state?
- What about retirement?
- What kinds of retirement program should I plan to offer long-term, loyal employees?
- What else do I need to know?

Your overhead, or fixed expenses, is the amount of money you have to have each month, even if you don't see one patient or make one sale of a concierge membership. These fixed expenses include rent, utilities, insurance, phone, and administrative salaries.

There is a term you should become familiar with—your *cash burn rate*. This is the amount of cash you spend each month. This can be different from your fixed expenses, depending on what you spend on variable expenses. This can include equipment, marketing consulting, temporary help, and so forth.

There are also variable expenses, which are the amounts you spend based on how many office visits, procedures, or concierge memberships you sell.

Other terms you must understand include the following:

**Revenue:** The amount of money received from sales.

**Income:** The amount of money from any source, including money from loans or as a result of investments.

**Profit:** Money you have remaining after deducting all your costs. There are two kinds, gross and net profit. The *gross profit* is the money that remains after deducting the cost of goods sold, but before deducting general and administrative expenses. The *net profit* is the amount you have after deducting the cost of goods sold, sales costs, and operating expenses.

**Net Loss:** The amount you may be short after deducting all expenses from all revenue. That's not good, but sometimes it happens, so start thinking about building a cushion.

Many times, businesses borrow money to launch. This can be a source of stress and anxiety. Try to rely on your own credit and your own money to be the primary source of funding. If you feel you need a cushion, consider a line of credit that you can tap and pay back quickly, and use only what you need.

The Small Business Administration says that personal credit cards are the number one source of financing for small companies. Expect to use your personal credit, and give personal guarantees for many business-related purchases or credit needs. If your credit is shaky, take steps to get it cleaned up before you endeavor to change to concierge medicine and transition your practice. The better your credit looks, the easier it will be to work with vendors, landlords, and lenders.

Pay your bills on time, every month. Your internal reputation from the staff suffers when they start to get calls from creditors about overdue bills from the business.

## Setting up Your Bookkeeping System

Your books can be something as simple as a spreadsheet, or a software program such as QuickBooks or Quicken. Your accountant will help you with your classification system, called your Chart of Accounts, and tell you which bills go into each category.

## Establishing Your Prices

Figuring out how to price your services in healthcare is not easy. I'll share a little secret. It is difficult in every service business. In concierge medicine, you really don't want to develop a brand as the low price leader because you'll only be able to go *down*. When I work with clients, they often start with this strategy in mind: "Sell lower than all the other concierge doctors, and give more." That's simply not sustainable and it doesn't bode well for your brand. Low prices don't always make up in volume for smaller profits. Plus, any competitor that can tolerate more risk than you, can undercut you. Then what?

Your brand should be established to be considered a premium brand. Your brand must be one where people get more because they pay more.

People don't shop concierge medicine by the lowest common denominator in price. They shop trust, location, and perception of value. Unlike the lower-priced general merchandise store, you can't put merchandise on special each week for loss leaders.

If you list out everything you want to include in your concierge membership amenities, how much will it cost if everyone takes you up on your offer? For that you must know your cost to operate your practice by the hour and by the service. Then you must add your profit margin in. When you offer an unlimited service like a concierge medicine amenity, your rate-limiting factor is your time.

Also, you want your business to grow, but if it grows too fast, will you be able to scale in a sustainable way? Or will you need more help?

While you may be tempted to charge similar fees to others, in the market, if your product is different, your fees should be different too.

During this phase, you will also need to open a bank account. Dig out your corporate papers file, because you will need to draft a bank account resolution for your corporation that says you give yourself the authority to do so. It seems silly, yes. But that's how it is done. The resolution looks like the example in Figure 15.1.

Try to select a bank that offers you a way to scan checks to deposit them with your smart phone or tablet so you don't have to spend time going to a bank to make deposits. Also consider setting up a credit card acceptance and credit-card-on-file program. The ability to accept both credit and debit cards makes life easier on everyone. So few people still carry a checkbook.

To set up a merchant account, contact your bank, and also Square and Paypal's new system called Here. I use both. They supply you with a little attachment for an iPhone or Android device that enables the card to be entered or swiped on transactions at checkout. There are several arguments in favor of this: First, you receive payment immediately. Second, the credit card company takes the risk of nonpayment. Third, you'll need to send fewer bills and statements or spend money on labor and postage to do billing. Don't forget that there is a small transaction fee, so plan for that in your pricing formula. There is also a discount fee of 2–4%. Costco offers a program to its executive members that is lower than many other options. Be sure to check that out. In some programs, there are monthly minimums you must meet and an administrative fee, as well as equipment to read the cards

**RESOLUTION TO OPEN BANK ACCOUNTS**

WHEREAS, the Board of Directors has determined it to be in the best interest of the Corporation to establish a banking resolution with (name of bank) be it:

RESOLVED, that the Corporation execute and deliver to said bank a duly signed original of the completed banking resolution as is annexed thereto, and that the authority to transact business, including but not limited to the maintenance of savings, checking and other accounts as well as borrowing by the Corporation, shall be as contained in said resolution with the named officers therein authorized to so act on behalf of the Corporation as specified hereto.

The undersigned hereby certifies that he/she is the duly elected and qualified Secretary and the custodian of the books and records and seal of (your business name), a corporation duly formed pursuant to the laws of the state of (your state) and that the foregoing is a true record of a resolution duly adopted at a meeting of (board or members) and that said meeting was held in accordance with state law and the Bylaws of the above-named Corporation on (date), and that said resolution is now in full force and effect without modification or rescission.

IN WITNESS WHEREOF, I have executed my name as Secretary and have hereunto affixed the corporate seal of the above-named Corporation this (day) of (month), (year)

_______________________________ (The name of the Secretary)
Secretary.

**Figure 15.1 Corporate Bank Account Resolution template.**

(free with Square and Here), and sometimes you may face chargebacks from customers who are dissatisfied with something.

Also, the manner in which you accept card payments may have a bearing on the percentage charged for the transaction. If a customer transaction is "card present," the fee is generally lower than if you accept it by phone or fax. It has been my experience as a practice administrator that the differential is negligible when attempting to collect on past due accounts because you can offer to take a credit card payment by phone instead of waiting for the check in the mail.

# Chapter 16

# Financial Forecasts and Budgets

Generally, physicians are the type of people either fascinated with numbers or daunted by them. Many small business owners are in these two camps. The numbers in financial reports reflect past decisions but are not the decisions themselves. They are the effect of the decisions. If you can forecast how much money you will make each month in medical services, concierge membership fees, and product sales (if any), you will be able to produce a budget that tells you how much you will be able to spend on rent, staff salaries and your own salary, equipment, and other business expenses for your practice.

Here's a budget challenge for new marketers and trade shows: If you market your concierge practice by exhibiting at a home show or wellness event, most people allocate the money to pay for a stand, but every stand has decorations, backdrops, posters, materials, and giveaways. There are also fees for setup because union members are the only ones permitted to drayage in some states. (*Drayage* is the transportation of things over a short distance. At conferences, drayage is the charge for the labor required to receive, store, and deliver freight to your booth or exhibit location, remove, store, and return empty containers, remove shipments from booths and deliver to the loading area of exhibit hall, where they will be loaded on common carrier trucks.) There are lots of rules associated with conference sponsorship and booth rentals, and each one of them seems to have an associated cost, all in addition to the booth or stand rental. They can unravel a marketing budget quickly if you aren't careful.

Another budget monster is marketing mailings. We are so used to the free sending of emails. To send to people who don't have computers or use them like a lifeline, design for print is very different than design for the web. Printing costs vary by source and the time line, and then there's the postage and the sorting service, and the mailing service. If you use stock photographs, there's the license based on the type of use you will have for the photographs.

So often, transition consultants want to send two or three mailings to your existing 3,000–4,000 patients. The postage for those mailings is often more than a letter. At present, first class letter mailings are $0.49, so a mailing to your patients will include the costs of design and layout, composition, printing, envelopes, stuffing, sorting, and postage. Each mailing could cost you $3,500. Even if you captured all 300–600 patients for a concierge membership max, what is the cost per conversion? Many of the consultants I've spoken with want to design three mailings, and send them out to all 4,000 patients. That's a commitment of $10,500 for three mailings. I know a few doctors who have agreed to do it, and their return on investment (without the payment to the consultant for the brilliant idea) was three to four membership purchases, total. Sorry, but I can come up with many other ways to spend $10,500 to attract fewer than five customers. That's a customer cost of over $2,000 per customer. No wonder their conversion estimates are in the $250,000 range.

It's difficult to create a real budget when you don't have all the facts. But start thinking about your marketing budget because that will be a tough challenge in the beginning until you learn what works.

## Exercise 1: Marketing Budget

| | *Monthly 1st Year* | *Total 1st Year* | *Monthly 2nd Year* | *Total 2nd Year* | *Monthly 3rd Year* | *Total 3rd Year* |
|---|---|---|---|---|---|---|
| **Professional Assistance** | | | | | | |
| Consultants | | | | | | |
| Ad Agencies | | | | | | |
| Direct Mail Specialists | | | | | | |

| | *Monthly 1st Year* | *Total 1st Year* | *Monthly 2nd Year* | *Total 2nd Year* | *Monthly 3rd Year* | *Total 3rd Year* |
|---|---|---|---|---|---|---|
| Graphics Design | | | | | | |
| **Brochures/Leaflets** | | | | | | |
| **Signs/Billboards** | | | | | | |
| **Displays** | | | | | | |
| **Samples/Giveaways** | | | | | | |
| **Media Advertising** | | | | | | |
| Print | | | | | | |
| TV | | | | | | |
| Radio | | | | | | |
| Online | | | | | | |
| Video | | | | | | |
| Other Media | | | | | | |
| **Phone Directories** | | | | | | |
| **Advertising Tchotchkes** | | | | | | |
| Direct Mail | | | | | | |
| **Website** | | | | | | |
| Development, Programming | | | | | | |
| Maintenance/ hosting | | | | | | |
| App licenses | | | | | | |
| Artwork licenses | | | | | | |
| Software & modules | | | | | | |
| **Trade Shows** | | | | | | |
| Fees & Drayage | | | | | | |
| Travel | | | | | | |

*continued*

| | *Monthly 1st Year* | *Total 1st Year* | *Monthly 2nd Year* | *Total 2nd Year* | *Monthly 3rd Year* | *Total 3rd Year* |
|---|---|---|---|---|---|---|
| Shipping | | | | | | |
| Exhibits & Signage | | | | | | |
| Promo Tchotchkes | | | | | | |
| Door prizes | | | | | | |
| **Public Relations Materials** | | | | | | |
| **Informal Marketing and Networking** | | | | | | |
| Membership/ Meetings | | | | | | |
| Entertainments | | | | | | |
| **Other** | | | | | | |
| **Grand Totals** | | | | | | |

Another worksheet you'll need to become familiar with is the Profit and Loss Projection. Let's have a look.

## Exercise 2: Profit and Loss Projection

| *Item* | *Months →<br>Add Columns<br>for Each Month Ahead* |
|---|---|
| **INCOME** | |
| Gross Sales | |
| (–) Paid Out Commissions for Marketing (if any—don't forget managed care write-offs) | |
| (–) Returns & Allowances (if any) | |
| **NET SALES** | |
| (–) Cost of Goods Sold (if any) | |

| **EXPENSES** | |
|---|---|
| Salaries and Wages | |
| Employee Benefits | |
| Payroll Taxes | |
| Professional Services | |
| Marketing and Advertising | |
| Rent | |
| Equipment Rentals | |
| Maintenance | |
| Depreciation | |
| Insurance | |
| Telephone Service | |
| Utilities | |
| Office Supplies | |
| Postage and Shipping | |
| Travel | |
| Entertainment | |
| Other | |
| Other | |
| Other | |
| **Total Expenses** | |
| Net Income before Taxes | |
| Provision for Taxes on Income | |
| **NET PROFIT** | |

And one more, your Cash Flow Projection. If you have two businesses, say one for CPT medical services, and one for your concierge amenities product and all things not covered by insurance programs, you'll need to do one each.

## Exercise 3: Cash Flow Projection

| *Year* | *Months → Add Columns for Each Month* |
|---|---|
| **CASH RECEIPTS** | |
| Gross Sales | |
| Cash Sales | |
| Collections | |
| **Total Cash from Sales** | |
| Income from Financing (if any) | |
| Interest Income | |
| Loan Proceeds | |
| Equity Capital Investments | |
| **Total Cash from Financing** | |
| Other Cash Receipts | |
| **CASH DISBURSEMENTS** | |
| Inventory (if any) | |
| Operating Expenses | |
| Sales Commissions/Returns & Allowances | |
| Capital Purchases | |
| Loan Payments | |
| Income Tax Payments | |
| Investor Dividend Payments | |
| Owner's Draw (if any) | |
| **TOTAL CASH DISBURSEMENTS** | |
| **NET CASH FLOW** | |
| Opening Cash Balance | |
| Cash Receipts | |
| Cash Disbursements | |
| **ENDING CASH BALANCE** | |

Now that you have these numbers, you can begin to consider writing a business plan. Without realistic numbers, you can't present them in a business plan and you can't borrow money from the bank or other sources.

What if you don't intend to borrow money from outsiders? You still need a business plan, you just don't need a big expensive formal one. Business plans are great as road maps. There are excellent books on business plan development, so I won't go in that direction for this book.

After you develop the business plan, or have a consultant develop it for you, you'll need another one of those resolutions of the corporation to go to the bank to say you are authorized by the corporation to borrow (or even apply to borrow) money. Use the template in Figure 16.1.

One thing to consider is, which corporation will be responsible for the debt? The new concierge corporation or the existing practice that does medical services (if there is one)?

RESOLVED, that the (person/role) of the Corporation is authorized, for the account of this Corporation, and on such terms and conditions as he/she/they may deem proper, to borrow from _ (named Financial Institution) sums of money; and to sign, execute, and endorse all such documents as may be required by said bank to evidence such indebtedness; to discount or rediscount with said bank any of the bills receivable owned by this Corporation; to apply for and obtain from said bank letters of credit, and to execute agreements to secure said bank in connection therewith, to pledge and/or mortgage any moneys on deposit or any moneys otherwise in the possession of said band, and/or any bonds, stocks, receivables, or other property of this Corporation, to secure the payment of any indebtedness, liability, or obligation of this Corporation to said bank whether now due or to become due and whether existing or hereafter incurred, to withdraw and/or substitute any property held at any time by said bank as collateral, and to sign and execute trust receipts for the withdrawal of same when required; and generally to do and perform all acts and sign all agreements, obligations, pledges, and/or other instruments necessary or required by said bank.

The undersigned hereby certifies that he/she is the duly elected and qualified Secretary and the custodian of the books and records and seal of (Your business name), a corporation duly formed pursuant to the laws of the state of (your state) and that the foregoing is a true record of a resolution duly adopted at a meeting of the (members/shareholders) and that said meeting was held in accordance with state law and the Bylaws of the above-named Corporation on (date of meeting), and that said resolution is now in full force and effect without modification or rescission.

IN WITNESS WHEREOF, I have executed my name as Secretary and have hereunto affixed the corporate seal of the above-named Corporation this (date).

______________________________

The Secretary

**Figure 16.1 Resolution to borrow from a designated bank.**

# Index

**Note:** Page numbers ending in *f* refer to figures. Page numbers ending in *t* refer to tables.

## D



## E



## F

## M



## N

## Q



## R

For Product Safety Concerns and Information please contact our EU
representative GPSR@taylorandfrancis.com
Taylor & Francis Verlag GmbH, Kaufingerstraße 24, 80331 München, Germany

www.ingramcontent.com/pod-product-compliance
Lightning Source LLC
LaVergne TN
LVHW080652011026
849160LV00014B/1403

* 9 7 8 1 4 6 6 5 6 8 1 8 1 *